EMPIRE WITHOUT TEARS

EMPIRE WITHOUT TEARS

America's Foreign Relations

1921–1933

Warren I. Cohen

Michigan State University

ALFRED A. KNOPF NEW YORK

FOR

BERNARD WISHY

THOMAS J. PRESSLY

RICHARD W. LEOPOLD

and

KATHERINE KINNEY

First Edition
987654321
Copyright © 1987 by Newbery Award Records, Inc.

Library of Congress Cataloging in Publication Data

Cohen, Warren I.
  Empire without tears : America's foreign relations,
1921–1933.

  Bibliography: p.
  Includes index.
    1. United States—Foreign relations—1921–1923.
2. United States—Foreign relations—1923–1929.
3. United States—Foreign relations—1929–1933.
I. Title.
E785.C64   1987   327.73   86–20876
ISBN 0–394–34145–7

Manufactured in the United States of America

Cover photo credit: Library of Congress

Cover design: Katherine Von Urban

Text design: Susan Phillips

PREFACE

I wrote this book to meet a need I perceived as a teacher. I teach a course on the foreign relations of the United States since 1919 and devote two to three weeks to events between 1919 and 1933. With classes too large to assign readings in the library, what are the students to read? I have found Robert A. Divine's *Reluctant Belligerent* and Walter LaFeber's *America, Russia, and the Cold War,* both in this series, extremely useful for the 1930s and the Cold War. The several paperbacks I tried for the 1920s simply did not work. The treatment of the "Republican era" in standard texts does not seem informed by the literature of the last twenty-five years and especially of the last decade. So I took time from my work on American–East Asian relations to prepare a short book for my class. I hope other teachers will find it as useful as I have.

My emphasis on the extensive involvement of the United States in the world affairs of the 1920s may offend the sensibilities of a generation educated in the 1940s and 1950s— perhaps even some of those trained in the 1960s. I realized in writing my first book, *The American Revisionists,* that the 1920s were too important to be dismissed as an isolationist interlude separating the internationalism of Woodrow Wilson from that of Franklin Roosevelt. The reader will find no reference to isolationism in this book. I trust my interpretation of the period will be greeted with a healthy skepticism and the kind of debate we all love in the classroom. I hope some readers will be tempted to explore a few of the books mentioned in the bibliographic essay.

ACKNOWLEDGMENTS

Three of my friends in the Michigan State University Department of History—John Coogan, Donald Lammers, and Peter Levine—made good faith efforts to improve the manuscript. Chris Rogers of Knopf obtained five thoughtful and detailed reviews for me. Robert A. Divine, editor of the series, provided excellent advice on revisions. Barbara Allyn, assisted by Ross Gardner and Dr. Victoria Kingsbury, may have learned to use a word processor as she typed the manuscript.

The work of several scholars has been especially helpful to me. A series of brilliant articles, books, and lectures by Michael J. Hogan, Melvyn P. Leffler, and Joan Hoff Wilson have helped enormously in the areas most remote from my own research. John Braeman and William Appleman Williams, perhaps an odd couple, both wrote important articles on the 1920s.

Bernard Wishy, my severest critic when I was an undergraduate at Columbia, said yes when, after tiring of premed and prelaw, I asked him if I might become a historian. Tom Pressly, by his example, taught me that teaching was far more than performing in front of a class. Dick Leopold was wonderfully encouraging during my early years in the profession—and spoiled my children. Finally, I would like to take this opportunity to welcome Katherine Kinney into the family. Thanks to her, I won't need the royalties from this book for Geoff's tuition.

CONTENTS

INTRODUCTION

In the quarter of a century preceding Warren G. Harding's inauguration as president of the United States, his country had emerged as a great power. It was a nation whose influence spread rapidly throughout the world. It controlled an empire that included not only the Caribbean basin, but stretched across the Pacific, north and south, through Hawaii and Alaska, Midway, Wake, Guam, Samoa, and the Aleutians, to East Asia and the Philippines. Manufacturers nurtured markets and sired multinational corporations in Europe, while mining and lumber interests scoured North and South America. American entrepreneurs and missionaries wandered across the Middle East, South Asia, and Africa. It was the dawning of what Henry Luce would later call the "American Century."

Although the United States was slow to develop military power commensurate with its industrial capacity, it did indicate a willingness to test its might. At the turn of the century Americans fought a war with Spain in which military units operated successfully in two oceans. American troops stationed in the Philippines engaged in a bitter struggle against Filipinos who preferred freedom to Yankee rule and participated in an international expedition against China in 1900. In the years that followed, the United States maintained military garrisons and naval units in the Philippines, China, Hawaii, and in its rapidly acquired Caribbean protectorates. President Theodore Roosevelt sent the Great White Fleet around the world, and the nation participated in an increasing number of international conferences, reflecting expanding interests and concerns. Ultimately, in the strongest testimony to

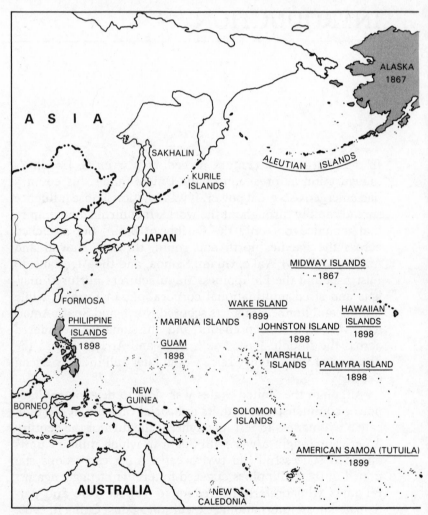

The American Empire in the 1920s

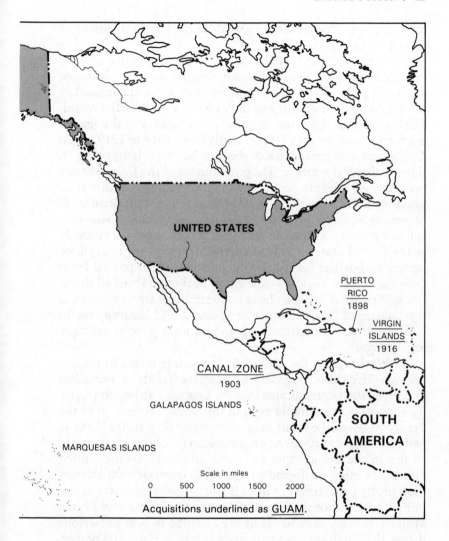

their growing involvement in world affairs, Americans went to war in Europe in 1917.

Prior to 1917, despite the efforts of publicists like Brooks Adams and Alfred Thayer Mahan, despite Roosevelt's use of his "bully pulpit," few Americans were aware of the impact of the world on their country or their country's role in the world. The world war shattered popular complacency and engaged mass attention. From 1914, certainly from 1917 to 1919, more Americans were concerned about what was happening in Europe than ever before. The government of the United States became more deeply occupied with international affairs than likely or even possible in time of peace. The American military establishment grew enormously, and its power was projected overseas. American financial power grew enormously as the United States was transformed from debtor to creditor nation and as the financial center of the world passed from London to New York. As new vistas beckoned from all directions, Woodrow Wilson chose to commit the United States to the League of Nations—to a permanent and leading role in world politics, consistent with the nation's power, prestige, and interests.

In Washington, the United States Senate failed to muster the two-thirds vote necessary to ratify the Treaty of Versailles and bring the United States into the League—although majority support was available even in the Senate. Rejection of the Treaty of Versailles and lack of membership in the League had little impact, however, on American involvement in world affairs in the decade that followed. In the 1920s the United States was more profoundly engaged in international matters than in any peacetime era in its history. The empire was maintained, with minor modifications in the Caribbean and China. Military power, as is usual in the absence of war or serious threat, declined—but never to prewar levels. Financial power, on the other hand, grew at nearly geometric rates, and the dollar, if not the flag, could be found wherever the sun might shine at any given moment.

EMPIRE WITHOUT TEARS

CHAPTER 1

WARREN HARDING'S AMERICA—AS RECEIVED

I

Writing about the government of the United States as it appeared at the turn of the century, the historian Robert Wiebe was struck by its failure to respond to "external reality." The apparatus for managing foreign problems was primitive, and initiatives were left to private interests and foreign powers. The Department of State was an amateur operation, and its overseas posts were a dumping ground for hungry politicos and wealthy young men indulging in brief resistance to joining the family business. The most obvious instruments of power, the army and navy, were decrepit. Wiebe found that "the paraphernalia for action simply did not exist."[1]

The apparatus Warren Harding inherited in March 1921 was radically different. It included a professional foreign service; a Department of Commerce geared to meet the needs of booming overseas trade and investment; a modern army (complete with general staff) more than twice the size of any force the United States had ever before fielded in peacetime; and a navy at least arguably the most powerful in the world.

Demand for an efficient, first-class foreign service was generated by those elements in American society most eager to assert American influence and power in the world. Businessmen, who began to organize in the 1890s, believed that improvement in American representation abroad would facilitate the expansion of trade. Others, associated with Theodore Roosevelt, Henry Cabot Lodge, Brooks Adams, and the "large policy" group, viewed the quality of their country's dip-

1

lomats and the buildings in which they worked abroad as indications of America's will to compete in the international race for glory. Roosevelt's ascent to the presidency allowed the process of reform to begin. Before he left office, the number of personnel within the Department of State had doubled, the number of foreign secretaries was growing rapidly, examinations were required for admission, and merit became the basis for promotion. Shortly afterward, in the Taft administration, the foreign service was completely reorganized. The reforms included the introduction of a training period for new officers, the establishment of geographic divisions, and a student interpreter corps for China and Japan. Congress not only funded all these changes, but appropriated additional sums for the first purchases of embassy and legation buildings. The United States was creating the "paraphernalia for action" of which Wiebe wrote.

World War I contributed further to the growth and professionalization of the foreign service. At the war's end there were five times as many diplomatic secretaries abroad as there had been in 1898, and five times as many people—officers, clerks, messengers, and janitors—working for the Department of State in Washington. Academic training for careers in international relations, including the foreign service, spread across the country. In 1906 no major American university offered specialized courses in world affairs or found much space in its curriculum for the study of countries outside Europe. By 1909 a wide range of such courses was offered at leading American schools. Nearly thirty such programs existed in 1916, and there were seventy by 1921.

All through the 1920s and into the early 1930s, the process of preparing young Americans to administer the world more efficiently continued. The first separate school of world politics was established by Georgetown University in 1919, followed by the Williamstown Summer Institute in 1921, the Johns Hopkins University School of International Affairs in 1925—the same year the Foreign Service opened its own school—and the Fletcher School of Law and Diplomacy in 1932. The marketplace indicated a need for more experts on foreign policy, and the universities proved responsive.

In 1922, Charles Evans Hughes, Harding's secretary of

state, contended that the department's workload had doubled since 1917. Much of the new burden involved economic affairs rather than issues of war and peace. American overseas trade and investment increased in quantity and complexity. Greater economic, military, and political power enabled the United States to cast an enormous shadow on the affairs of the world in the development of international communication networks, in the reconstruction of war-ravaged economies in Europe, and in the development of the resources of undeveloped economies in Africa, Asia, Latin America, and the Middle East. The Foreign Service was compelled to cope with such issues, especially in Europe, where governments intervened increasingly in matters most Americans believed best left to the private sector. But the Department of State had help —indeed competition—in the handling of economic diplomacy from a revamped Department of Commerce.

The Department of Commerce, like State, was deeply indebted to turn of the century concerns among businessmen fearful of being unable to compete with Great Britain and especially Germany in world markets. Indeed, the very existence of the Department of Commerce, created in 1903, derived from a perceived need to rationalize American efforts by facilitating greater cooperation between business and government. By 1912, the department had established a Bureau of Foreign and Domestic Commerce. Woodrow Wilson's aggressive secretary of commerce, William C. Redfield, had been president of the American Manufacturers Export Association. He lobbied successfully with Congress for additional appropriations, opened branch offices around the country, and created a corps of commercial attachés—all steps designed to expand opportunities for foreign trade.

During World War I, major American businessmen mobilized to move enlarged capital reserves into areas long dominated by European interests. A leading historian of American business, Mira Wilkins, called the war "a watershed in the history of multinational enterprise."[2] New direct investments poured into less developed regions, especially in Latin America, and especially through export-oriented firms. The American International Corporation, created in 1915, involved giants such as U.S. Steel, General Electric, the National City

Bank of New York, and the Rockefeller family. Initially created to lend to the Allies, the organization also planned for postwar investment and export development, with encouragement from Redfield and his most illustrious successor, Herbert Hoover. Congress was responsive to such efforts, passing the Webb-Pomerene Act in 1918 and the Edge Act in 1919. The first allowed exporters and the second banks to enter into combinations, exempt from antitrust laws, to facilitate foreign trade.

When Harding appointed Hoover secretary of commerce, the direction in which the association of government and business would proceed was already clear. Hoover reorganized the department, with special attention to the Bureau of Foreign and Domestic Commerce, and quickly gave businessmen the efficient service they had come to expect of him. Hoover saw exports as essential to business stability and national prosperity, but he was no less alert to problems faced by importers of commodities whose source was controlled by foreign governments. Like Hughes at State, Hoover provided his department with superb leadership. In economic as in political foreign policy, the nation was better prepared for taking on the world than it had ever been.

The American military was not to prosper in the 1920s like the nation's diplomatic and commercial apparatus. In general, neither American leaders nor the people were willing to use force to expand the empire. Expansion would come by peaceful means, especially economic. Nonetheless, Harding inherited a formidable military establishment—large, modern, and combat hardened. The traditional pattern of rapid return to peacetime status and dismantling of the military machine did not prevail after World War I. To be sure, the army was demobilized rapidly, but the National Defense Act of 1920 left the general staff with a sufficient number of officers for planning and provided the first permanent assignment to plan for industrial mobilization in time of war. Army leaders now thought in terms of total war and had to consider the possibility of sending troops overseas again. General John J. Pershing's appointment in 1921 as chief of staff enhanced the staff's prestige and he developed a War Plans Board for operations planning. By 1923 the army had its first peacetime mobilization plan and an Army Industrial College designed to prepare officers for the problems of industrial mobilization.

In the initial postwar years, the navy fared even better. Before the United States intervened in the war, Wilson's attitude toward naval building programs changed radically. By December 1915 he was advocating the creation of a fleet second to none. The office of Chief of Naval Operations (CNO) was also established in 1915. In 1916 Congress passed a Merchant Marine Act containing subsidies designed to stimulate the growth of the merchant fleet. After the United States declared war, the navy quickly found itself with more men than any fleet in existence. And apparently, wartime practices proved habit-forming. When the war was over, Wilson asked Congress to continue naval building and offered a new supplementary program that, if completed, would have given the United States a navy more powerful than all existing navies together. Congress stinted a bit, but gave Wilson enough so that he left to Harding a navy which in ships built and in process was considerably larger than the British in capital ships, destroyers, and submarines. The naval historian George T. Davis has noted that "the United States built in the three years after the Armistice many more ships of war than the rest of the world combined."[3]

Harding even inherited an air force. It was not much and it suffered disproportionately during the postwar demobilization, but it had grown from one pilot in 1910, to 8 in 1911, to 20,000 army and navy pilots at the end of the war. As part of the army, in the early 1920s the Air Service dropped to about 10,000 officers and men working with nearly 3,000 planes, mostly obsolescent. Nonetheless, the nucleus for creating modern air power was there when Congress became more responsive to the arguments of men like Billy Mitchell in the late 1920s.

The point, of course, is that when the Harding administration took office, the United States was the leading power in the world, with the accoutrements of power and the wealth and apparatus to expand it. The nation was geared for the expansion of American influence and interests abroad and in the 1920s precisely that occurred, on an enormous scale, unprecedented in American history.

II

In 1914, American investors surpassed the efforts of their British competitors only in Mexico, Cuba, Panama, and at times elsewhere in the Caribbean basin. Throughout the rest of the world, wherever foreign business was present, the British or occasionally other Europeans were dominant. The pattern changed radically in the 1920s, setting the stage for American economic hegemony before World War II. In 1914 the United States was a debtor nation, owing foreign investors $3.7 billion more than was owed to Americans investing abroad. By 1919, a sharp reduction in foreign investment in the United States and wartime loans to the Allies had transformed the United States into a creditor nation, with a favorable loan balance of approximately $3.7 billion.

The growth of private economic power, of surplus capital in the United States, was not lost on President Wilson. In 1915 he was troubled by his inability to aid China during the crisis occasioned by the notorious Twenty-one Demands Japan presented to the Peking government. Realizing that the demands were designed to give Japan political as well as economic control, Wilson tried to persuade American bankers to invest in China's modernization. With the president's support, his minister to China, Paul Reinsch, worked frenetically to interest American businessmen in Chinese projects, hoping to spare China the consequences of dependence on Japanese loans—to which political strings were always attached.

In 1916, Wilson realized that one aim of the Paris Economic Conference of that year was European and especially British retention of control of the postwar international economy at the expense of the United States as well as those powers that found themselves among the vanquished. Wilson and his advisers objected to British plans for preferential systems that would deny American businessmen access to markets or raw materials not only within the British Empire, but also among sterling bloc traders like Argentina. Denied equal opportunity to compete, Americans could hardly be faulted for seizing wartime opportunities to replace British dominance with American.

While the president's desire for national prosperity and the businessmen's quest for corporate profit appeared congruent, other engines drove American economic expansion after 1914. As the United States prepared for war and then fought, the government needed "strategic" commodities, like rubber and nitrates, and urged businessmen to find and develop assured sources. Similarly, alarms about an oil shortage at the end of the war prompted government support for overseas exploration and concessions. The result was a dramatic challenge to European dominance throughout the world which Congress tried to facilitate with legislation like the Webb-Pomerene and Edge acts and to which the executive branch gave diplomatic support—most clearly in the demand for unconditional most-favored-nation treatment for Americans everywhere. The early successes of the challenge led American businessmen to realize that Europe's hold could be broken—feeding corporate imaginations, and probably greed as well.

Some prominent American businessmen and President Wilson stressed the interdependence of world economies and had reservations about a purely competitive model for American involvement in the postwar world. Wilson had always favored cooperation on reasonable terms and the League of Nations, as he conceived it, was fundamentally an instrument for international economic and political cooperation. His approach had strong support on Wall Street, particularly among the partners of J. P. Morgan and Company. Morgan had branches in London and Paris, had worked well with Allied financiers during the war, and had every intention of continuing cooperative arrangements. In 1919 and 1920, Thomas W. Lamont, J. P. Morgan, Jr.'s public persona, was asked by the Wilson administration to create a new four-power banking consortium to enable the United States to cooperate with Great Britain, Japan, and France in the financing of China's modernization. Presumably the agreement which Lamont succeeded in negotiating would enhance the possibility of stability in East Asia while protecting China from Japanese extortion and increasing opportunities for American investment.

By 1919, American foreign direct (as opposed to portfolio) investments had increased to an estimated $3.9 billion, an increase of nearly 50 percent over 1914. American investors were moving toward a leading role in the Western Hemisphere, including Canada, where British investors fell behind for the first time in 1922. But Africa and Asia remained out of reach, and critical raw materials like nitrates, rubber, and tin were still controlled almost exclusively by Europeans. There was much to be accomplished in the 1920s.

When Harding took office, a worldwide depression had dampened investor ardor. Nonetheless, the pattern for creating American hegemony in the 1920s was clear. When possible, the United States would cooperate with other nations in the development of the resources of Asia, Africa, and Latin America and of markets throughout the world. Where Europe or Japan tried to exclude American interests, superior American economic power would be brought to bear. The main instrument of economic expansion, whether cooperative or independent, would be private business. It would have the support of government in protecting home markets, gaining access to scarce raw materials, and forcing doors for trade and investment.

Harding's advisors, especially Hughes and Hoover, were alert to the dangers and the opportunities. They—particularly Hoover—differed from Wilson primarily in their greater reluctance to use political or military means to maintain and expand the empire. Wilson had created a powerful military to complement America's new wealth, and that military was implicitly a club which would assure American leadership in the new world order. In the 1920s, military power was allowed to atrophy. There would be few American boys fighting for the empire: it would be an empire without tears. (I use "empire" throughout to encompass two very different manifestations of American wealth and power. First, I use the term in the traditional sense of territories controlled, directly or indirectly, by the government of the United States, including China, where the privileges of empire were shared with other powers through the multilateral imperialism of the treaty system. Second, I use "empire" in the less than universally accepted sense of "informal empire," to include cases in which the principal instruments for the control of other peoples or their resources are private, generally economic, and profit-motivated, in which the role of the U.S. government is secondary or nonexistent. Those who are its objects rarely distinguish between the exercise of official and private American power.)

III

If the informal economic empire did not penetrate the consciousness of Americans quick to condemn European or Japanese imperialism, the United States also maintained extensive holdings in the form of colonies, protectorates, and territories. In these more obvious evidences of imperialism, American government officials ruled openly as in the Philippines or less formally as in most of the Caribbean protectorates. Like the other symbols of American power, most of the physical empire had been acquired since the late 1890s. But the process had begun much earlier.

Of all the empire as Warren Harding inherited it, Alaska had come first—a frozen wasteland inhabited by an alien race and remote from the contiguous and united states, with little prospect of ever gaining statehood. Military government gave way to civil government in the 1880s. The Klondike Gold Rush in 1896 resulted in sufficient permanent American settlers to gain territorial status by 1912. Perhaps someday Alaska might be a state after all.

Congress and the public resisted further expansion for most of the rest of the nineteenth century. The major turning point was the Spanish-American War, after which the question of whether the United States would become an openly imperialist power was widely debated and answered in the affirmative. Hawaii, a focus of annexationist efforts since the 1850s, became American territory in 1898 and was granted local self-government in 1900. Its racially mixed population was anathema to most Americans, and its chances of entering the union on a basis of equality with the continental states were slim indeed. Before the year was out, the United States had added Puerto Rico, Guam, and the Philippines to its noncontiguous possessions. Guam was placed under naval jurisdiction, and the army fought to suppress the Filipinos until 1902. Puerto Rico immediately obtained civil government, power resting with a governor appointed by the president of the United States. U.S. citizenship was granted during the Wilson years, as was a greater degree of self-government, but there was no indication of future autonomy or independence. The Philippines were promised eventual independence, but power to govern remained in the hands of men appointed by the president of the United States.

The empire continued to grow, but public and congressional opposition or indifference precluded the systematic development of a colonial administration or colonial office within the American government. Moreover, traditional anti-imperialism required that the empire be disguised and rationalized. Hints of eventual statehood for Alaska, Hawaii, and Puerto Rico would ease some consciences, however remote the reality. The promise of eventual independence for the Philippines, after appropriate tutelage, soothed others. Finally, the concept of "protectorate," clearly not a colony, facilitated American hegemony in the Caribbean.

Beginning with Cuba, the administrations of McKinley, Roosevelt, Taft, and Wilson established American protectorates throughout the region. Panama, which would not have existed without American support, fell into this category in 1903. Roosevelt, assisted by U.S. Marines, added the Dominican Republic in 1905, and Taft acted similarly with Nicaragua in 1910. Wilson, contemptuous of the imperialism of Roosevelt and Taft, maintained American control over all their acquisitions, and used American marines to include Haiti in 1915. Although the practices of imperial management differed from place to place, in each instance there was a diminution of the sovereignty of the country involved and special rights and privileges for the United States. An American military presence and control of the customs houses was common.

By 1921 the United States also possessed Tutuila in the Samoan Islands of the Southwest Pacific and the Virgin Islands in the Caribbean, the former obtained by treaty dividing the spoils with Germany in 1899 and the latter purchased from Denmark under threat of seizure in 1916. American garrisons could be found throughout the empire, most notably in the Caribbean where the marines maintained some semblance of order in the Dominican Republic, Haiti, and Nicaragua. Bases were being developed at Guantanamo Bay in Cuba and the Canal Zone in Panama. A chain of bases and military installations, some admittedly more potential than real, existed across the Pacific in Hawaii, Tutuila, Guam, the Philippines, and on the mainland and in the territorial waters of China. The flag may not have been as omnipresent as the dollar, but it was getting around.

IV

During the World War, the American government, through the efforts of the Creel Committee (Committee on Public Information), undertook an unprecedented campaign to sell to the world the cultural values dominant in the United States. Shortly after the war ended, the government ceased to play a role, but American cultural involvement continued to expand. The missionary goal of the "Christianization of the world in this generation" may have fallen significantly short of the mark, but the Americanization of the world in this century did not seem incredible in 1921.

Beginning in 1919 and continuing to the mid-1920s, there was an enormous increase in the number of Americans who volunteered to serve abroad as missionaries and an equivalent increase in contributions to support missionary activity. Missionary-supported universities flourished. If the war had taught little else, it had persuaded some Americans that the rest of the world was in desperate need of the progressive values that had catapulted the United States into a position of world leadership. Young and old, Americans stepped forward to sacrifice the comforts and safety of home to teach Africans, Arabs, Asians, Latin Americans, and even the French about the blessings of Protestant Christianity, democracy, free enterprise, and modern sanitation. Many eventually returned with a better understanding of the outside world and of the national aspirations of the people among whom they worked.

Similar sentiments led to the creation of the great American philanthropic foundations and to their overseas programs. Shortly before the war, Andrew Carnegie had created the Carnegie Endowment for International Peace and financed the building of the Peace Palace at the Hague. He committed his trustees to ending war and then to doing whatever else was necessary to "aid man in his upward march to ...perfection even here in this life." The Carnegie Endowment financed peace organizations at home and abroad and ran a center for European peace in Paris. Not to be outdone, John D. Rockefeller created the Rockefeller Foundation in 1913 and ultimately financed an American cultural presence around the world, notably the Peking Union Medical College in China.

On another level was the spread of organizations like Rotary International, a service organization for businessmen. Originating in Chicago in 1905, it opened hundreds of chapters across the country and then, after the war, expanded rapidly abroad. Its 1921 convention was held in Edinburgh, Scotland. By 1929 it had nearly as many chapters outside the United States and Canada as it had altogether in 1920. Everywhere it propagated the idea that the businessman, dedicated to service, could bring peace and prosperity where politicians and diplomats had failed.

Rather a different set of American ideas were offered around the world by itinerant scholars. As America emerged as the leading world power, developing countries eager to find the key to wealth and power turned increasingly to it. At Peking University, Ch'ên Tu-hsiu, subsequently founder of the Chinese Communist party, invited John Dewey to lecture. For a year, Dewey's ideas had the opportunity to capture the imaginations of Chinese intellectuals who would lead their nation in the decades to follow.

Perhaps the most effective overseas cultural involvement of the United States was the motion picture. During the war, American filmmakers shot far ahead of potential European competitors and dominated mass markets in the years that followed. In the early postwar years, in Great Britain and France as well as in Canada and Latin America, Hollywood portraits of American life and Hollywood's canned values prevailed. From 70 to 90 percent of the movies shown in those areas were made in America.

In the churches, hospitals, universities, and movie theaters around the world, the American presence was felt as Woodrow Wilson prepared to vacate the White House in honor of Warren Harding. These were symbols of American wealth and power and, more to the point, symbols of American interest in projecting American ideas and values to the rest of the world.

V

The political culture of the United States in 1921 also reflected an interest and involvement in international affairs unprecedented in peacetime America. The war had stirred the peace movement to greatly intensified and increasingly sophisticated activity. The struggle over ratification of the Treaty of Versailles had focused much of the historic tension between executive and legislative branches on foreign policy issues. Participation in the war and in the peacemaking bred a group of experts on world affairs who formed the foreign policy "establishment." Harding's cabinet contained at least two men, Hughes and Hoover, who had spoken for their party on foreign affairs issues in the past and perceived a leadership role for the United States. For all Harding and his constituency's longing to return to "normalcy," there could be no retreat from the rest of the world for the generation of the twenties. The search for order, so pronounced in the Progressive era, had become a search for world order.

The American peace movement consisted of a score or more organizations committed to the vision of a world at perpetual peace. Some of the organizations dated well back into the nineteenth century; others emerged in the course of the Great War. A few had substantial memberships, but most consisted of a director or executive secretary, a few office assistants, and, with luck, an impressive board of directors to list on the letterhead. Some had strong religious doctrines to guide them; others were secular. Most of the organizations accepted the existing international system of nation-states, but a few pressed more radical programs for world federation. Almost all had offered strong support for the idea of a League of Nations. By 1921, however, the same fissures that divided the Senate divided the peace movement. Agreement could not be reached on sanctions, although there was considerable acceptance of economic as opposed to military sanctions. Some pacifists could accept no form of coercion.

In the battles over the League in 1919 and 1920, peace movement leaders and their followers divided over Article X of the League Covenant. Even within the League to Enforce Peace, the organization most closely associated with the idea of an international organization, members divided along party lines. The majority, who were Republicans, supported Republican Senator Henry Cabot Lodge's reservations to the Democratic president's treaty. With the third defeat of the Treaty of Versailles in May 1920, however, all the peace organizations were committed to finding a way for the United States to take the lead in organizing the world for peace. In particular, many movement leaders were apprehensive about the rapid growth of the U.S. Navy and fearful of militarism in the United States. Something had to be done to divert funds from military spending to more humane and progressive ends. Disarmament and particularly naval arms limitation interested most of the peace groups. Some were attracted particularly to the idea of membership in the World Court. A few hoped to be able to outlaw war, and the League of Nations Association was created to keep alive hope of American membership. All seemed persuaded that the United States had a special mission to lead a benighted world in an age without war.

The peace movement found allies in Congress, notably Senator William Borah of Idaho. One of the Irreconcilables, villains in the League fight, Borah was a bundle of inconsistencies on foreign policy issues, but the staunchest congressional supporter of arms limitation and outlawry of war efforts, as well as a fierce critic of most aspects of American imperialism. With Borah dominating debate on foreign policy issues, as well as succeeding Lodge as chairman of the Foreign Relations Committee, the possibility of American membership in the League vanished. On the other hand, the administrations of the 1920s faced restraints in military spending and the use of force in dealings with foreign countries that delighted peace activists. Borah's extraordinary presence was clearly a mixed blessing for the peace movement, but together they shaped the milieu in which policy was formulated in the 1920s. No president, no secretary of state could act without an eye on Borah and the movement.

Another organization indicative of increased interest and involvement in world affairs, the Council on Foreign Relations, was incorporated in 1921. Its founders, including Thomas Lamont, welcomed the rise in public interest in world affairs, hoped to foster it during the postwar years, and to provide expert knowledge—leadership—to a people traditionally occupied with domestic concerns. Elitist in conception and membership, the council functioned apart from the peace movement, although council members often shared the goals of peace organizations and contributed to them. The council represented what came to be known as the "foreign policy establishment"—bankers, lawyers, academics with professional interest in world politics, collectively with access to presidents and secretaries of state far greater than that of the peace organizations. Many of its members were "in-and-outers"—men whose careers alternated between government and private sector positions. In general, council members worked with the executive branch and peace groups found it easier to influence congressmen. Probably the most important distinction between the Council on Foreign Relations and the peace movement was the willingness of most council members to countenance the maintenance and use of American power. There were few if any pacifists among them.

The generation of American leaders that experienced the World War was determined to prevent another such atavistic explosion. The men who came to power in March 1921 differed little from the Wilsonians in their commitment to peace. But in rejecting the League, Wilson's device, the Harding administration would have to sustain its commitment in some new way. Harding, in his campaign and in his inaugural address, had spoken vaguely of "an association of nations," presumably an alternative to the League, but nothing ever came of that vapid idea. Hughes and Hoover had promised that a vote for Harding was the surest path to the League, but had not the power to make good the promises. Harding's most valuable contribution was his sensible deference to Hughes, with whom Hoover competed modestly.

Hughes was the most prestigious member of the Harding cabinet, overshadowing even the president. He was a distinguished lawyer, associate justice of the Supreme Court, and had been only narrowly defeated for the presidency in 1916. He had favored American membership in the League, but it had not been his cause. Other means of having the United States play a responsible role in world affairs could be found. He considered himself a progressive and was convinced that order was fundamental to progress. As a lawyer and jurist he had an intellectual and emotional commitment to legal approaches to maintaining order at home and abroad. While not unaware of the role of power in the affairs of nations, he may have underestimated its importance. His own disinclination to build and use national power was reinforced by the postwar public mood in America. Hughes was sensitive to public opinion, particularly as a source of limits on the government's power to act effectively. Without public support, the government could not long sustain any given policy. He thought in terms of a need to educate the public, as did his friends on the Council on Foreign Relations. Others thought him occasionally timid, fearing to take appropriate action lest Borah or the peace movement be provoked.

In this setting, there emerged what the historian Richard Leopold has called the "interwar compromise."[4] The central question for the 1920s was how to stay out of war, preferably while increasing the benefits Americans enjoyed from expanding involvement in world affairs. A minority, strongly represented by the Council on Foreign Relations and the League of Nations Association, argued that the United States could not avoid being drawn into a second world war. Once such a war started, American participation was inevitable. The only way to keep the United States out of war was to cooperate with other nations for the preservation of peace, most obviously through membership in the League or at minimum, cooperation with Britain and France.

Most people with views on American foreign policy in the 1920s had a simpler solution: The United States could stay out of future wars as an act of will. It had intervened voluntarily in 1917—next time it would not, even if all of Europe and Asia were at war. Borah, representative of much of this thinking, was convinced that the key to peace for America was to avoid obligations or commitments that might lead to war. He and many of those who shared his outlook were unwilling to surrender the overseas interests of the United States, but insisted on looking after those interests independently. They favored a course another historian, Joan Hoff Wilson, has labeled "independent internationalism."[5] When foreign policy was an issue in the 1920s, there were few advocates of an American retreat from world affairs. Rather, the debate was between a minority that advocated collective security and a majority that rejected collective security as the best means to preserve the American empire without war.

In the 1920s the United States attempted to pursue an independent policy, compromising frequently to cooperate with other nations for specific purposes. The policies of the era were epitomized by agreements with other nations on an ad hoc basis, to solve specific problems. Commitments, except to consult, were carefully avoided, as were provisions for enforcement, for sanctions if the agreements were violated. A generation aware of the tendency of post-1945 America toward overcommitment might see the policy of the 1920s as timid, but what is really striking is the increased participation of the United States in major developments around the world, compared with the role the nation played prior to 1917.

CHAPTER 2

THE USES AND IMPACT OF AMERICAN ECONOMIC POWER, 1919-1929

I

The decade of the 1920s, at least the seven or eight years between the recession in which Harding found the nation and the stock market crash that marred Herbert Hoover's first year in the White House, has long been recognized as an era of striking economic growth in the United States. Industrial production rose 70 percent between 1922 and 1928. In the same period the gross national product (GNP) rose 40 percent, per capita income 30 percent, and real wages 22 percent. The growth was notable because it occurred not in what would later be called euphemistically a "developing country," but in a nation that was already the world's leading industrial power. If Calvin Coolidge actually insisted that the business of America was business, the large majority of Americans benefitting from a mass economy that turned out enormous quantities of affordable consumer goods were quite content. This was "people's capitalism": Business leaders allowed wages to rise, took their profit in the volume of sales, and displayed social consciousness. Businessmen were the folk heroes of the decade. In their Rotary Club speeches and songs, they stressed their service to the community. Public relations men like Bruce Barton sold Jesus to the people as the greatest advertising man of all time—just as Moses was the greatest real estate promoter.[1]

Generally, businessmen found the government of the United States cooperative to a greater degree than ever before, eager to promote the interests of American business at home and abroad. Historians have labeled the America of the 1920s the "cooperative" state or the "promotional" state, while recognizing that many—perhaps most—of the innovations of the twenties began during the world war. Moreover, in capitalist America the historian would be hard pressed to find an era in which government did not seek to cooperate with and promote the interests of American business—especially in its dealings abroad. What might be different about the 1920s was the "associational" activity—and philosophy—the theory and practice of government business cooperation for the general interest that sometimes blurred the lines between public and private sector operations. The use of Thomas Lamont, the Morgan partner, on a series of quasi-governmental missions beginning in 1920 is the most striking manifestation of the new process.

Although in the 1920s government seemed unusually responsive to business and the public uncommonly worshipful, there remains the fact that the business community did not speak with one voice. On a few issues like collecting debts owed by the Allies to the U.S. government and nonrecognition of the Bolshevik regime in Russia, there was near unanimity. On a host of other issues, suppliers often differed from producers, exporters from importers, and international bankers from most everyone else. At least in part as a result of these divisions, the peace movement probably had more influence over foreign policy issues than did the business community.

Perhaps the central tension not merely within the business community but also within the government, and unresolved in the minds of some individuals, derived from the desire to maximize American economic opportunities at a time of growing awareness of economic interdependence among the leading market economies. The earliest indications of the problem came in the shaping of war debts and tariff policy. During and immediately after the war, Allied governments borrowed more than $10 billion from the United States. At the peace conference the debtor nations had proposed cancellation of the debt, arguing that the money had been spent in the common cause and that they had contributed lives for which there could be no repayment. Wilson, alert to the certainty of congressional opposition, refused. Presumably for the same reason, he rejected Allied suggestions that their debts to the United States be linked to reparations due them from Germany. Lamont and others argued that refusal to cancel or scale down substantially would affect European reconstruction adversely and inevitably depress the American economy. but to no avail. Renewed British efforts in 1920, including an offer to waive repayment of money they had lent—in excess of what they owed the United States—as part of a general debt settlement were rejected by Wilson.

Hughes and Hoover understood the economic issues, the interdependence of European and American prosperity. Lamont did not leave that to chance. Politically, however, the issue was too difficult to handle. Congressmen heard their constituents clamoring for tax relief. They had no desire to undertake the burden of explaining the value of the tax increase that cancellation would require. The argument that the average American would benefit more from cancellation, which would presumably stimulate exports, and increase corporate profits and employment rates in the United States, required more faith in the system than congressmen dreamt of finding in their districts. Indeed, the dominant pressures exerted by businessmen on their representatives were in favor of increased tariff protection. Protection of industries and markets developed during the war took precedence over strictures about interdependence and cooperation. As a result, the first major economic action of the new administration was the Emergency Tariff Act of May 1921—immediate relief to business from the low tariff policies of Wilson's southern Democrats—and increased difficulties for Europeans who had to sell in American markets to get the dollars with which to repay their debts.

Clearly Congress restricted the freedom of action of the Harding administration, like the Wilson administration, in achieving a sensible resolution of the war debts question. On the other hand, there is nothing to suggest that, left to their own devices, Hoover and Hughes would have favored cancellation. The refunding arrangements for which they eventually won congressional acquiescence—and which ultimately resulted in a de facto cancellation of 50 percent of the debt—

represented the limits of their own obeisance to the gods of interdependence. They, differing little from most organized business interests, wanted to see a reconstructed European market—without accepting a significant tax burden and without risking the enhancement of Britain's competitive position. They wanted a financially stable Europe, which they perceived as the key to a peaceful Europe, without jeopardizing their vision for a stronger domestic economy. Hoover was persuaded Europeans could repay much of their debt and, for all his understanding of interdependence and the need for cooperation, was still committed, ultimately, to a world economy in which the United States was dominant. In short, the war debt problem of the 1920s derived less from ignorance than from a desire to maximize America's competitive position while attempting to create a world economic order based on cooperation and an equitable distribution of benefits. The would-be architects, Hoover foremost among them, were unwilling to choose between goals foreign leaders would insist were irreconcilable.

Throughout the 1920s, American pressure on its former allies for debt payment and Allied, especially French, demands on Germany for reparations troubled the economic relations of the industrial world. The French were willing to use force to collect from Germany, and the Germans kept borrowing from American banks to meet their payments while revitalizing their economy. In 1925 and again in 1929, major new funding arrangements allowing Germany to avoid default were devised by American businessmen. Charles Dawes and Owen Young, architects of the Dawes (1924) and Young (1929) plans, were ostensibly private citizens, but both were appointed by the government of the United States. The government had much to do with the implementation of both plans, especially with stimulating American bankers to provide the necessary loans. The most obvious point is that the American government, in the course of the world war, had undertaken the role of international lender on an unprecedented scale, which role required it to become involved in the financial affairs of Europe to an unprecedented extent. Hughes, Hoover, and Andrew Mellon, the secretary of the treasury, were intensely concerned about the stability of the franc and the mark. However much it tried to avoid involvement in European affairs, the United States government could not. Some American leaders accepted the expanding involvement willingly, others grudgingly. But there was no turning back.

II

American trade statistics in 1921 were not impressive. The wartime economic boom collapsed in 1920 as the nation struggled ineptly with the problems of reconverting to a peacetime economy. Imports dropped off sharply, followed soon thereafter by a decline in exports. Nonetheless, the auspices were good. Europe had begun the task of reconstruction after a devastating war. In Asia and South America, major development projects were underway. Everywhere there was a strong demand for American machinery and industrial products. The obvious dilemma was how to provide would-be foreign customers with the dollars they needed to purchase American goods without allowing them to sell more of their own goods in the United States. The United States was enjoying a favorable balance of trade and there was little inclination to tamper with that pleasant statistic.

Lamont and other bankers had warned that insistence on raising tariffs to restrict imports and collection of war debts would leave Europe without the means to purchase American goods for reconstruction. If the international bankers had their way, war debts would have been canceled or greatly reduced, import restrictions would have been rolled back, *and* the government of the United States would have lent money to European governments for purposes of reconstruction. Lamont may well have been the most powerful private citizen in the country, but he could not sell his program in Washington. He was one war ahead of his time.

Despite tariff increases in 1921 and 1922, imports began to rise again in 1922, sending dollars abroad—although not nearly enough to finance the potential export trade. The shortage was covered by tourism and loans from the private sector. Foreign travel by Americans increased greatly in the 1920s, with approximately 80 percent of the fares going to foreign carriers. At the peak in 1929, nearly 400,000 Americans traveled to Europe, Asia, and South America. In addition to supporting British, French, and other non-American ocean liners, American tourists spent billions of dollars abroad in the 1920s. Still, Europeans, Japanese, Chinese, and Latin Americans needed more dollars. As demand drove interest rates up, Lamont and his colleagues were increasingly willing to bridge the gap. Between 1919 and 1929, foreign loans floated in the United States totaled approximately $7.5 billion—more than the total provided by all other capital-lending countries combined. And so the American export trade grew.

In the early 1920s and as late as 1924–1925, agricultural sales to Europe were unusually high, reflecting the temporary needs of that war-ravaged continent. Thereafter, agricultural exports declined continually, especially wheat and pork. In general, the war had rescued American farmers from the deteriorating competitive position in world markets evident since the Populist era. On the other hand, raw cotton remained the leading American export item throughout the 1920s and well into the 1930s. The striking exception to the larger trend was the export of fruit, which continued to increase, doubling between 1923 and 1929.

As European farmers reclaimed lands and replaced livestock, the importance of Europe as a purchaser of American exports declined. From 1921 to 1925, Europe purchased 53 percent of what the United States sold abroad. By 1929, the European share of the American export trade had dropped to 45 percent. The decline can be attributed entirely to reduced agricultural purchases, since Europeans continued to buy approximately one-third of the finished manufactured goods exported from the United States.

It was, of course, in manufactured goods that American exports soared. In 1914, the infant automobile industry exported cars and parts valued at $34.6 million. In 1920 total sales were valued at over $303 million. A sharp drop in 1921 proved temporary, and sales soared again in 1925, reaching a total of $541.4 million by 1929. Machinery sales abroad increased from $168 million in 1914 to $607 million in 1929. The export of petroleum and petroleum products rose from $161 million to $561 million over the same period. Iron and steel sales increased over 200 percent. Even in rubber products, American exports were up over 600 percent, thanks to the manufacturers of rubber tires. As productivity increased, as the automobile industry led the nation to prosperity in the 1920s, exports, especially automobile-related exports, increased the American share of the world's imports. The United States had become the world's leading exporter, responsible for 15.6 percent of the world's total in 1929.

Europe, especially Great Britain, Germany, and France, continued to be the best market for American goods. Canada was second only to Britain as a customer. In the 1920s, for the first time, Japan rivaled France for fourth place on the list. Led by Japan, Asia began to increase in importance as a market, purchasing approximately 12 percent of American exports over the years 1926 to 1930, compared to 5.6 percent for 1910 to 1914. And everywhere the trader went, representatives of the Departments of State or Commerce—or both—did what they could to ease the way.

On occasion, the government of the United States took initiatives designed to overcome the apathy of businessmen in countries like China. For several decades, publicists had waxed eloquent about the potential of the China Market, but trade continued to be disappointing, averaging about 1 percent of American exports in the five prewar years of 1910–1914. The last effort of the Wilson administration, the re-creation of the four power banking consortium designed to lend money to the Chinese government, had seemed promising. But Lamont, who had negotiated the agreement at the behest of the U.S. Department of State, disappointed his government in the years that followed by finding myriad excuses for denying loans to China. No more or less a patriot than the next businessman, he and his Morgan partners were more interested in the highly profitable, low-risk loans they could extend to Japan than they were in stimulating Chinese-American trade or the investments of American industrialists—in other people's profits. J. P. Morgan and Company, he might have said, was not, after all, an eleemosynary institution.

Frustrated by the inactivity of the consortium and the marginal improvement in American exports to China, Hoover promoted several China trade acts designed to facilitate trade and investment. These acts provided federal incorporation for participating companies and exempted them from most federal taxation. More than 70 out of approximately 500 American firms functioning in China took advantage of the law, but neither trade nor investments ever reached the levels of which publicists and officials dreamed. In the 1920s China lacked the stability and the Chinese people lacked the purchasing power necessary to attract substantial American investment or to buy very many Fords.

In a very different way, the U.S. Departments of Commerce and State were more successful in helping American businessmen. Import restrictions were the province of Congress; the executive branch could take little credit or blame. Exports were facilitated modestly by commercial attachés and diplomats and by legislation which allowed associational activities, free from antitrust prosecution, for companies in the export business. Perhaps most important were the efforts to assure American industry access to strategic materials like oil and rubber.

Immediately after the world war, there was a widespread perception of an oil shortage. The Wilson administration had fought hard to protect the nation's interest in oil supplies and the opportunities of American companies to exploit oil resources in the Middle East, East Asia, and Latin America. The Harding and Coolidge administrations shared these concerns. Certainly Hughes and Hoover were agreed that the United States had a strategic interest in remote oilfields and that an assured supply of oil was central to the vitality of the American economy. The oil companies, on the other hand, were less interested in supplying American needs than in maintaining and expanding their worldwide marketing outlets. Nonetheless, oil company executives and diplomats, with assistance from the Department of Commerce, worked together to gain concessions in Venezuela, Iraq, Bahrain, Kuwait, and the Dutch East Indies. Representatives of the American government appeared in nominally unofficial capacities at a series of international conferences touching on concession disputes; American diplomats argued with their European, Latin-American, and Middle Eastern counterparts; and Hughes and

Hoover attempted to impose guidelines on oil industry executives who entered into actual agreements. No one could fault
the American government for the energy it expended, nor was
there any doubt that the men in Washington were confident
their activity was in the national interest, as opposed to the
particularistic interests of the oil companies.

Rubber was another commodity that worried Herbert
Hoover. In 1922 the British were troubled by falling prices
that adversely affected their colonial holdings. They devised
the Stevenson Plan, a system of price supports, to reduce production and restrict exports. The United States was the consumer most affected: 70 percent of the world's rubber was
used in American industry, especially the automobile industry. For six years Hoover and the British sparred, much to the
irritation of both sides. Hoover protested to the British, supported Firestone's effort to develop an independent source of
supply in Liberia, persuaded bankers not to lend money to the
rubber or any other cartel, and fought unsuccessfully for legislation to exempt companies buying from cartels from antitrust legislation, allowing them to form buyer combinations.
The British did not yield to Hoover's pressure. They demanded tariff reductions Hoover could not deliver as the price
for increasing rubber production and ending export restrictions. What Hoover could not accomplish, Dutch-controlled
rubber plantations did achieve. The Dutch refused to participate in the Stevenson Plan and began to capture previously
British markets. In 1928, the plan was dropped.

Commodity cartels were clearly a danger to the United
States, which had become the world's principal consumer of
primary materials. Americans were the largest users of every
important metal and an extraordinary range of other raw
materials. Here was another way countries like Britain,
France, and Germany could obtain dollars with which to purchase American goods or put pressure on the United States for
concessions on tariffs or war debt payments. These nations
tried to control the sources of the raw materials, either on
their home soils or in their empires, driving up prices and
squeezing American consumers. Like the Wilsonian free traders before him, Hoover considered government-supported

commodity cartels an outrage and fought them with every means at his disposal.

After the world war, the United States became the world's leading exporter and ran Great Britain a close second in the race for leading importer. Of raw materials, the United States was the world's largest consumer and importer. Unquestionably, Americans had an enormous impact on the economies of other countries and were in turn affected by the practices of other countries. The American economy was very much a part of the world economy and in the boom years of the 1920s, prosperity in the United States was dependent in part on assured access to raw materials and to markets for American products. It was therefore important to develop a foreign economic policy that would sustain a world economy in which the United States fared so well. Obstacles to markets or raw materials had to be eliminated, and dollars had to be available to those who would buy American goods.

The government of the United States was not successful in creating a coherent, sensible foreign economic policy. There were ideological obstacles that limited the role the government could play, as with the unwillingness to have the U.S. Treasury lend Europe money for reconstruction. There were political problems that precluded an optimum solution to the war debts problem or the creation of an ideal tariff. As always, special interests resisted a government purporting to act in the general interest, as when bankers subverted efforts at loan controls. And, of course, there were problems of ignorance and inexperience, of failing to comprehend the nation's new role as creditor. But Hoover certainly, Hughes, and Frank B. Kellogg, his successor at State, at least arguably, understood the need for Washington to play a larger role in world economic affairs, to provide direction at home and leadership abroad.

III

In the course of the 1920s, many billions of dollars were transferred from the United States to other parts of the world. Among the various methods were imports, remittances (usually cash sent to relatives in the old country by recent immigrants), tourism, and investments, both direct and portfolio. All these were ways of keeping the dollar in motion, keeping the world economy operating by giving foreigners the means to purchase the produce of American factories and farms. The government played an important role in two of these activities, imports and investments. Tariff laws restricted imports, providing the United States with a handsome balance of trade surplus—and the rest of the world with deficits. Tariff reduction was anathema to Republican stalwarts and thus not readily available to aspiring economic planners. Portfolio investments, specifically in the form of loans, became Hoover's principal target, as he tried to use the visible hand of the Department of Commerce to adjust the mechanisms of a market economy.

Capital flowed out of the United States from 1919 to 1929 in quantities without precedent in the world. Approximately $12 billion dollars went abroad, mostly in the form of loans —and most of that long-term loans to debtor nations. Demand for American capital was intense throughout the decade despite high interest rates. Europeans needed dollars to purchase American goods needed for reconstruction, and they borrowed regardless of cost. The rest of the world, which traditionally turned to European bankers, had no alternative in the 1920s but to queue up in Wall Street.

Despite sometimes chaotic, often unstable conditions in some of the borrowing countries, investment bankers were willing to float loans, and Americans were willing to subscribe. Lip service was paid to the patriotic duty to lend as outlined by government, industrial, and banking sources eager to sustain export markets. What really attracted bankers and investors was the chance for unusual profit provided by high interest rates. Investors knew there was some risk involved, but most borrowers had good repayment records and there was very likely an expectation that the power of the United States government would chasten any potential defaulter. For the bankers, the commissions came with the sales of the bond issues, and the least scrupulous worried little about how wasteful the loans might be or whether they would be repaid. They were still playing with other people's money.

The system that developed was inherently unstable. The whole international economic system of the 1920s came to depend on the outflow of long-term loans from the United States to maintain a balance between the supply of and the demand for dollars. A major default could change American investment patterns and bring about the collapse of the world economy. A form of loan control designed to protect the investor and permitting only such loans as promised to be most productive might have helped avert disaster. Of course, a more conservative loan policy would have meant fewer dollars available to purchase American goods—unless the tariff was revised to allow more imports. Joan Hoff Wilson has argued that "only strong loan control *in conjunction with* lower tariffs, increased imports on the part of the United States, and cancellation of the outstanding intergovernmental debts would have changed the world financial situation before 1929."[2] While not claiming such policies would have averted the Depression, Wilson does suggest that it would have been less severe.

Herbert Hoover came close to understanding these questions and worked stubbornly, but with limited success, to gain control over foreign loans. He does not seem to have recognized the need for integrating economic, political, and military policy. Nonetheless, he did have a vision of creating a more productive and peaceful world through the sensible use of American capital. Loans should never be allowed for the purpose of building a nation's military establishment, either directly or by making it possible for other funds to be diverted for military use. His principal concern, however, seemed to be the effectiveness of a given loan. Would it contribute to the development of a country, to the development or reconstruction of its industrial infrastructure? Would it contribute to social stability, a condition he deemed essential to progress? Would it improve living standards, or consumer consumption? Would the money be used to strengthen the borrowing nation's productive capacity? If the answer to these questions was positive, Hoover also wanted assurance that the loan was sound, that investors were likely to be repaid and were informed about the risks. Finally, he wanted the loans to have clauses restricting the ways in which the money could be spent. In particular, Hoover wanted "buy American" clauses that would require recipients to use American supervisory personnel and purchase materials in the United States.

Opposition to Hoover's approach was pervasive. Bankers generally welcomed government involvement in international loans only when the government was intervening to collect on bad debts; they were not interested in being told in advance which loans were likely to end badly. Even the most enlightened international bankers, men like Lamont and Benjamin Strong, governor of the New York Federal Reserve, were opposed to federal controls, especially restrictive clauses. Andrew Mellon, secretary of the treasury, was willing to use loan controls as a club with which to collect war debts, but was not otherwise interested in meddling with the bankers. Hughes and Kellogg were interested in loan control as a political tool, provided the Department of State exercised the control. Ultimately, Hughes's position prevailed.

The idea of guidelines for foreign loans had come up during the Wilson administration. The Harding administration developed a set during 1921 and announced them in March 1922. Hughes was less interested in how loans were to be used abroad than was Hoover—other than being determined that they would not be used in a manner detrimental to American interests as he perceived them. In particular he was interested in using loan control as a way of reinforcing nonrecognition in bringing Mexico, the Soviet Union, and the banana republics to heel. Against the opposition of the bankers, the government announced that all foreign loans open to public subscription required prior submission to the Department of State, which would indicate whether the loan was objectionable. No law required the bankers to obey the secretary, but failure to comply and receive the State Department's imprimatur would hamper efforts to float a loan. On the other hand, State Department approval, despite Hughes's insistence to the contrary, implied the soundness of the loan and a government obligation to assist in the event of default. Hughes was aware of the latter complication, and very uneasy about being used by the bankers. He suspected *political* approval of loans was being deliberately misused by bankers to help sell bond issues to the public.

Ultimately, the role of the government in loan supervision proved to be surprisingly extensive, although the results were at best mixed. In the Caribbean, Big Brother had unusual powers. America's protectorates in Cuba, Haiti, and the Dominican Republic were required by law to obtain Washington's approval for new borrowing. The Department of State exercised a tight rein on these nations, but failed to prevent extraordinarily wasteful loans to Cuba, providing substantial wealth for the usual combination of investment bankers, corrupt officials, and landowners. It was difficult, and probably impossible, to ensure honest and practical use of the money once lent. Where Americans did have some control over local spending, they were generally too much concerned with the interests of the bankers. Efforts to preempt corrupt practices by blocking a loan to Panama resulted in Panamanian authorities turning to Canadian bankers. The Department of State was more successful with schemes in Guatemala and Honduras, apparently blocking efforts by American bankers that were manifestly exploitative.

Other examples of intensive American government involvement in loans and the world economy abound, most of them of greater political consequence. The infant Republic of Austria, a state created after the war without adequate regard for its economic viability, desperately needed funds for reconstruction. At the initiative of the British government, Lamont of J. P. Morgan and Company and Morgan's British partners, Morgan, Grenfell, working with Strong of the New York Federal Reserve and the Bank of England, worked out the necessary financing. American government officials watched over the negotiation and, eager for stability in Central Europe, approved the loan.

Efforts by Lamont and other American bankers to finance Japanese imperialism in Manchuria met occasional opposition from the Department of State, but the bankers had little trouble redesigning the loans to make them palatable. Japanese officials and financiers had grand schemes for developing East Asia using Japanese brains and American money. The Department of State preferred not to permit American capital to be used to the detriment of American entrepreneurs competing with the Japanese. The bankers, however, were interested in the profits assured by dealing with Japanese government-created entities like the Oriental Development Company and the South Manchuria Railroad. Their patriotism and will to assist their government did not extend to the point of sacrificing arrangements in their own interest to the interest of their countrymen.

Having placed itself in the position of having to pass on the desirability of foreign loans, the American government found itself in the awkward position of having to take a stand that would offend the Japanese government, whose goodwill it coveted rather more than that of Haiti or Guatemala. Always the ingenuity of the bankers prevailed. In 1922 the Department of State objected to a National City Company loan to the Oriental Development Company, fearing its use to further Japanese dominance of Manchuria, Mongolia, and North China. After the failure of other ploys, the Japanese government offered assurances that the money would be used exclusively in Korea, and the Department withdrew its objection. Efforts by the South Manchuria Railway to borrow in the United States were consistently thwarted, but the bankers simply lent money to other Japanese entities, where it was "laundered." Unquestionably in the 1920s American capital was used to extend Japanese control over Manchuria and to develop the Japanese overseas empire. The American government attempted on several occasions to prevent this, but failed.

In Europe American loans played their most important role, staving off what in retrospect appears to have been inevitable disaster. The central problem was that of German reparations, of which France was to collect the lion's share. The inability of the Weimar Republic to maintain payments led to a French and Belgian armed occupation of the Ruhr that lasted nearly two years, beginning in January 1923. In December 1922 Hughes attempted to head off armed intervention, suggesting the creation of an international commission of experts on which American financiers would be willing to serve. The British were interested, but the French, playing dog in the manger for most of the 1920s, had to learn the hard way. Passive resistance by the Germans in the Ruhr, the near collapse of German currency, and the sharp fall in the value of the franc led to greater French understanding. Lamont helped by refusing to float a currency stabilization loan for France until French authorities were prepared to behave more sensibly. Had he wanted to arrange the loan, it was clear that the Department of State would object. The bankers and the government, cooperating with their British counterparts as well, won their point. In late 1923, a commission was established chaired by Charles B. Dawes, a Chicago banker. In April the commission issued its report, known thereafter as the Dawes Plan. Its key provisions were a reasonable schedule of reparations payments by Germany and a $200 million loan to Germany to stabilize its currency and allow it to make the required payments.

With help from Hughes, who arranged to be in London at the time of a fifteen power European conference on the Dawes Plan, the plan was adopted in the summer of 1924. It took another year, until August 1925, to get French troops out of the Ruhr. Of the $200 million loan, $110 million or 55 percent was floated in the United States. And the American government stayed close to the issues, using its theoretical control of foreign loans to ensure the success of the Locarno Conference of October 1925, in which mutual guarantees of the Franco-German border were given and a sense of security, the "spirit of Locarno," allowed to rise however briefly over the continent.

The capital involved throughout this operation was private. American citizens participated in the arrangements without official government appointment. Nonetheless, the interest and the hand of the American *government* was apparent throughout. Indeed, Morgan and Lamont had reservations about the loan which Hughes volunteered to delay if necessary to allay their concerns.

Loans to the Weimar Republic flowed easily and steadily from the United States from 1924 to 1929. The public alone bought nearly $1.5 billion in German stocks and bonds, and American banks offered large advances to German banks. The German central government, state governments, and city governments floated loans in the United States. Major industries —iron and steel, electrical and chemical plants, railroads—all came to the United States to borrow. With American capital, the Germans rebuilt and expanded their industrial infrastructure. Some Americans were uneasy about the resurrection of German power, troubled by the strength of unrepentant German nationalists; but they comforted themselves with the knowledge that most Germans were peaceloving—and luxuriated in or dreamed of the profits the loans had and would continue to provide.

By late 1925, the Department of State noted that first claim to many of the assets Germany was offering as collateral for loans belonged to those nations owed reparations. As new loan issues were presented for clearance, the Department began to indicate its reservations to the bankers. The bankers reported that they saw no cause for concern: The Germans were paying their debts. Hoover was troubled by what he perceived as the danger of a major German default disrupting the American economy and pressed the Department of State. Kellogg, Hughes's successor, was unwilling to question new loans publicly, but in 1927 warned the German government that he would be forced to act if German borrowers did not show more restraint. The German government was at least minimally responsive and the capital flow diminished, although it did not stop before 1930.

Despite growing apprehension in Washington, the peaceful reintegration of Germany into the world community and the world economy seemed to have been accomplished by 1928. A rehabilitated Germany had joined the League of Nations and signed the Kellogg-Briand pact renouncing the use of force. The time seemed appropriate for an end to the postwar occupation and a final disposition of the reparations question. The American government concurred. It was eager to participate as a means of protecting its enormous stake in Germany, but unwilling to attend officially and risk having to confront the war debt issues. Once again a prominent businessman was selected as the American government's unofficial representative. Owen D. Young, chairman of the board at General Electric, a key figure in the commission that produced the Dawes Plan, accepted appointment by President Coolidge to head the new committee in January 1929. Young, were he acting on his own, would have included discussion of the war debts, but both Coolidge and president-elect Hoover instructed him to the contrary. Hoover was markedly displeased with the report of the Young Committee, but with help from Lamont, Young was able to persuade Hoover not to oppose the plan publicly. Again with Lamont's help, Young sold the plan to the essential European nations, all of whom had finally ratified it by May 1930, in the last hours before the collapse of the world economy, already signaled by the crash of the stock market in New York months before.

Looking back in early 1930, the loan supervision policy and the cooperative, "corporatist" relationship between Washington and Wall Street seemed to have worked reasonably well. Certainly the major international bankers had little to complain about. Unquestionably, they had accumulated great wealth. Those who, like Lamont, had worked closely with their government, were persuaded that they had transcended the interests of their firms and served not only the nation, but the well-being of the world. Lamont had worked with foreign governments, bankers, and industrialists, especially the British, in shaping public policy, in creating the foundation of a strong, reasonable, and enduring world economy. American capital was fueling the expansion of the economies of all the great and some not so great nations and it was all being done without resort to force, without tears.

In Washington there was rather less satisfaction. Hoover and Hughes and many of their subordinates were aware that the bankers were most cooperative when fortunes were to be made supporting the government's perception of the national interest. When pursuit of the national interest threatened profits, even Lamont proved to be strikingly evasive, even dishonest. Obviously Morgan and Company's preference for lending money to Japan rather than to China irked government specialists in American–East Asian relations, few of whom could match his access to the president and cabinet-level officers. But most important was the steady development throughout the decade of a government role in international loans—an awareness of the importance of these loans and of the inadequacy of market forces to serve American interests. The Departments of State, Commerce, and the Treasury had to collect information about the economies of dozens of nations around the world and make scores of decisions about the feasibility of loans. Officially or otherwise, the government of the United States had to participate in every major political or economic conference in the world to protect its interests. And as Hoover, in 1928, looked out over a world at peace and promised a chicken in every pot, a car in every garage, neither he nor his colleagues could have been too dissatisfied with the results of their efforts.

IV

There was, of course, another major outflow of capital that distressed Hoover intensely: direct investments leading to the development of American owned factories abroad. Hoover feared the United States was creating a monster that would take markets away from American industrialists and jobs away from American workers. Corporate boards, however, were less interested in Hoover's theories than in profit. More than $4 billion in direct investments were made in the 1920s. Direct investment in Europe doubled, and by 1929 there were more than 1,300 wholly owned or American controlled organizations there.

Many of Hoover's fears were realized. The largest investments were made in the most highly developed countries, where American companies became multinational corporations in the effort to expand their markets. Europeans wanted American products because of advanced American technology, but their governments erected tariff barriers to hold back the flood of foreign goods. In general they did not stop the flow of capital and technology, as American businessmen established branches abroad or wholly owned subsidiaries, or entered into joint ventures with local entrepreneurs. Much the same sort of development occurred in Canada and, to a lesser extent, in Argentina and Australia.

Companies selling processed foodstuffs, electrical equipment, automobiles and tires, and office equipment were most prominent abroad. Cars were produced in Canada and Europe by the Big Three for local sales. They eliminated the native industry in Canada. General Motors, through its control of Opel, dominated the German market. In England, Ford built the largest automobile factory outside the United States.

Ford also built assembly plants in Japan, Latin America, and Turkey. IBM and Remington-Rand built factories all over Europe. General Electric and IT&T were prominent in Europe, especially in England and Germany. In Canada, General Electric controlled the largest electric company and American subsidiaries produced more than two-thirds of Canada's electrical equipment. But outside the textile industry, there seemed enough jobs for anyone who wanted work in the United States. European governments rather than Washington were troubled by the invasion of American multinationals.

American oil companies invested huge sums in marketing operations, perhaps as much as half a billion dollars in Europe, and at least another quarter of a billion in Canada, Latin America, Asia, and Africa. In France, for example, the law penalized the importation of refined oil, so Jersey Standard built refineries in that country and sent in crude oil extracted elsewhere. In addition, American-based multinationals gained control of important public utilities all over the world. IT&T, created in 1920, was the dominant corporation in communications. By 1929 it had larger investments in communications than any competitor, foreign or American, and had more employees overseas than any other American firm. The American and Foreign Power Company, organized in 1923, controlled the power and light facilities of Shanghai, China's largest city. Although investment in railroad construction overseas declined, it soared in air transportation, with Pan American Airways activities in Latin America in the lead. American drugstores, five and dime, and grocery chains spread over Canada.

Most of this activity occurred with minimal involvement by the government of the United States. For the most part, major corporations that had little need for official assistance were involved. When government assistance was requested, it was often routine, and rarely of importance. The striking exception to this rule was the support Pan Am received from the U.S. Department of State. Viewing Latin America as a preserve to be controlled by the United States, the Department was eager to break European monopolies where they existed and consistently encouraged investment. Control of the air links was considered especially important if the United States was to gain regional superiority, and the Department wanted Pan Am rather than European airlines to dominate. The strategic value of controlling the airways received at least nominal consideration.

Over on the other side of the world, the Department of State was eager, as was Hoover at Commerce, to have American investors finance China's industrial infrastructure. The problem there, however, was not so much foreign competition as the indifference of the major international bankers, including Lamont. Corporations interested in communications, like Federal Telegraph, found Lamont and the consortium an obstacle rather than a help in raising funds for operations in China. The bankers were perfectly willing to allow Japan to dominate what they saw as high-risk investments in China, while they and most major corporations sought to put their money where they had reasonable assurance of friendly, stable governments. Efforts by the U.S. government to push investment in China were unsuccessful. In general, the multinational corporations had their interests, and the government of the United States had its interests. Although the interests overlapped on occasion, leading to professions of patriotic zeal on the part of businessmen and of concern for profits on the part of bureaucrats, they were never identical.

When it came to obtaining supplies, especially materials of apparent strategic importance, business and the government worked more closely together. As noted previously, Hoover was always ready to fight against supplier monopolies or cartels. The Department of State was always ready to demand access to oil or other raw materials essential to American industry. The traditional American demand for equal opportunity received at least ritual support from American diplomats everywhere.

The pattern of investment overseas for purposes of access to primary materials differed from that designed to develop markets. In particular, capital went to less developed countries rather than to Europe. It was heavily concentrated, however, in the Western Hemisphere, in Canada and Latin America. On the other hand, no continent was free of a direct investment by multinational corporations based in the United States. Even the colonies and dominions of the great European powers were penetrated. Moreover, whether involved in agriculture like United Fruit or extractive industries like mining or oil, the corporation that invested directly in less developed countries generally had a much greater impact on the local society than did the opening of an automobile factory in Europe or Japan. The great novelists Joseph Conrad in *Nostromo* and Gabriel Garcia Marquez in *One Hundred Years of Solitude* have depicted the rise of company towns in physically remote areas of Latin America, their contributions, and the problems they caused.

Mining operations attracted more capital than agriculture in the 1920s. The greatest increases in American investment were in Latin America, as the Guggenheims went after nitrates, copper, lead, zinc, and tin in Chile, Peru, and Bolivia, replacing British capital with American. The Guggenheims also challenged the British in Malaya and Northern Rhodesia (now Zambia). In Canada, the largest mining company, the International Nickel Corporation, producer of 90 percent of the world's nickel, was American-controlled. American capitalists even attempted to develop the mineral resources of Soviet Russia as Armand Hammer negotiated for asbestos concessions and Averell Harriman for manganese—without support from the United States government, which did not recognize the Soviet regime.

Although mining interests persisted in their efforts to extract profits from Mexico in the face of revolution, nationalist hostility, and nationalization of subsoil rights, oil men looked elsewhere, especially to Venezuela and the Middle East. Standard Oil of New Jersey gambled on the failure of the Bolsheviks, invested almost $9 million in Russia immediately after the war—and lost it all. In the Middle East, the Department of State was heavily involved in efforts to assist American companies competing with Europeans for concessions. Requiring more oil for their worldwide marketing outlets, the Americans persuaded the Wilson and Harding administrations of the danger of an oil shortage, of the importance to the national interest of Middle Eastern oil. Hughes offered diplomatic support in exchange for assurances that all American companies would have access to the new fields. The oil men agreed, but once the major companies won a share from the Europeans, they were quick to forget, quick to shut out other American companies. The most flagrant example of this tactic came in the Mesopotamian oil fields, where the American group of oil companies never had any intention of honoring its commitment to Hughes.

In agriculture, two companies stand out. Most important was United Fruit, which developed an enormous stake in Central America during the 1920s. Of all American corporations operating in foreign lands, United Fruit probably had the worst reputation for meddling in the internal affairs of host countries and disrupting the local society. Stated most simply, the company was far wealthier than the countries in which it functioned, and its operations sometimes overshadowed all other activity. In Costa Rica, United Fruit had a larger budget than the national government. In Honduras, revolutionaries obtained their funds from the company, which with another American fruit grower produced the bulk of the government's revenue. It bought huge tracts of land. Dependent as it was upon local conditions, dependent as local officials were on the company's operations, there was enormous potential for corruption. In general, United Fruit needed no help from the American government: It could buy whatever it needed locally—at least in the 1920s. The other agricultural operation of note was Firestone's development of its own source of rubber in Liberia in response to British efforts to restrict supplies in 1922. Firestone was eager for government support, received encouragement from Hoover, but never was able to persuade the Department of State to provide the desired diplomatic offensive.

In sum, the multinational corporations that mushroomed in the 1920s were an important part of the greatly expanded role of the United States in the world economy. Although their assets were multinational, most of the capital came from the United States, and the profits were distributed largely in the United States. However reluctant American officials were to meddle in the affairs of these corporations, they could not hide from the implications of corporate activities. However much the corporations resented government interference, good relations with Washington were worth cultivating in the event of complications with host countries. Washington generally preferred to leave the businessmen alone and the businessmen generally preferred to work alone, but there were shared interests in American prosperity, in American self-sufficiency in strategic materials, in enlarging the role of the United States in various parts of the world. A diplomat interested in China or the Middle East knew that his work would be perceived as more important and receive greater support from the public, Congress, and his superiors if an economic stake was developed in his region.

The relationship between the American government and the American-based multinational corporation seemed innocent enough in the 1920s. For the most part, Washington left dirty deeds to the private sector, and provided unexceptional, routine assistance. Only in the case of Pan Am in Latin America is there clear evidence that the government role was crucial.

Clearly, the impact of American trade, investments, and tourism on the world economy in the 1920s was enormous. No other nation even approximated the United States in economic importance. The British, who kept first place among importing nations, lost their preeminent investment role in Latin America and Canada, and were being challenged throughout Europe and the rest of the world, including their colonies, by American capitalists. The Americanization of the world was under way.

American products were appearing everywhere. Automobiles, electrical equipment, communications equipment, office equipment, and farm machinery were in great demand. Less obvious in the short run, although foreseen by Hoover, was the transfer of American technology abroad. Innovations that contributed to the rapid development and primacy of American industry were demonstrated in American-built factories in Europe, Japan, and Canada: mass production, standardization of parts, scientific management. The direction of development in preindustrial societies was influenced by American investments and travelers. In addition to their depredations, multinational corporations contributed significantly to public health programs, transportation, and housing as a means of providing a healthy and reliable work force. The Guggenheims had a good reputation for building schools in remote areas. Mira Wilkins has argued: The "Central American bananas, Chilean copper, and Venezuelan oil became valuable resources *only* because foreign companies were ready and able to take large risks, to supply sizable amounts of money, and to offer technical knowledge and skills"[3]—and those firms were largely American. No one would suggest that the corporations involved went abroad for charitable purposes. The point is that in their pursuit of profit they affected every society they touched, and some of these in very important and sometimes mutually beneficial ways.

The flood of American tourists affected the structure of industrial societies as well as less developed countries, stimulating the shipping industry, the hotel industry, and all the trades and services that exist to separate the affluent traveler from his or her money. Moreover, the income from the tourist traffic eventually moved through the local economy, providing a stimulus to the larger economy. At least $500 million and probably closer to $1 billion passed from American into foreign hands in the 1920s, as the citizens of the world's leading power flocked abroad to enjoy their new status.

In addition, the direction in which American money flowed sometimes determined which nations would progress and which would decay, which peoples would prosper and which suffer. Unconsciously, Americans were engaged in a form of triage. Investment capital was needed all over the world, and not enough was available. Those who could persuade the bankers to lend or the multinationals to build might gain wealth, power, even a chance to live. Those who failed faced stagnation, even death. In East Asia, for example, the bankers, working on the soundest of investment principles, chose to lend to Japan and not to China. As a result, Japan prospered, expanded its empire, tightened its control over parts of China. In China, the economy continued to decline, millions were underemployed, millions of others died from starvation or more directly from floods. American bankers did not create Japanese imperialism, but they found it profitable to strengthen it. American bankers were not responsible for civil wars, inadequate flood control, or food supplies in

China, but they might have been able to ameliorate those conditions and did not. When the United States became the primary source of capital in the world, decisions as to how that capital would be used affected the lives of hundreds of millions of people all over the world—of whom most Americans were never aware.

The American government played a very modest role in all these activities. Some Americans thought about a larger government role, of formulating a coherent, integrated foreign economic policy. Hoover, Lamont, and Young, though not in agreement among themselves, offered a range of ideas for Washington's intervention in the world's economic affairs. A few, like Hughes, had vague ideas about coordinating economic and political foreign policy. Little came of these thoughts in the 1920s because of conflicting interests, domestic political obstacles, and ideological rigidity. When a man like Lamont offered a program "in the national interest," it was always clear that the program was in the interest of his firm, and not always clear that it was indeed in the *national* interest. Other businessmen contested his views and few congressmen, farmers, or workers would have rallied to his support. Interest groups in the United States rarely unite on a conception of the national interest. Politically, congressmen were uninterested in tampering with tariffs that protected their constituents or with plans for canceling war debts that were likely to raise a furor among taxpayers. Ideologically, few American leaders were ready for the government of the United States to provide peacetime loans for reconstruction or development. As for government regulation of the flow of capital abroad, even the enlightened Lamont became apoplectic at the thought.

In the absence of a consensus among American leaders in and out of government on a specific program for foreign economic policy, the government muddled along in the usual way, promoting and assisting business as best it could. With a professional Foreign Service and high-powered Department of Commerce, that assistance was better than ever before. When major problems emerged abroad for which Congress or the American public was presumed unready to accept responsibility, the American government participated quietly, often unofficially, occasionally using a private citizen to disguise its role from its own people.

During the 1920s the government of the United States did not control the flow of American tourists abroad or the amount of money they spent. It did not control the investments of the scores of multinational corporations that spread their operations all over the world. It did seek some control over foreign loans floated in the United States, but this activity was of marginal importance. At no time in the 1920s did the government exercise effective control over American economic activity abroad. Economic policy was rarely an effective instrument of foreign policy. That is not the same, however, as saying that overseas economic activity had no impact on foreign relations. Regardless of the level of governmental involvement, American overseas economic activity had enormous influence on the world economy and the affairs of individual nations. In many parts of the world, American trade, investments, and foreign economic policy constituted the most important relationship with and for the United States.

CHAPTER 3

TOWARD THE PRESERVATION OF PEACE

I

In the era of Harding and Coolidge, the conventional diplomatic activity of the United States also intensified. Of particular importance were international efforts toward maintaining world peace. To American leaders, peace was not merely an intrinsic good; insofar as the United States was the leading beneficiary of the existing world order and best equipped to determine the shape of peaceful change, none doubted that peace was in the interest of the nation and its empire.

It would be wrong, however, to see American participation in conferences and agreements designed to strengthen the "peace machinery" of the world merely as the coolly calculated moves of shrewd statesmen, as *Realpolitik*. The horrors of the world war had shown Americans as well as Europeans what modern warfare was like. Few talked of its glories; few could wax as eloquent as Theodore Roosevelt had about the joys of what John Hay called that "splendid little war" back in the summer of 1898. The postwar literature, stories by William Faulkner, John Dos Passos, Ernest Hemingway, Erich Maria Remarque, Hermann Hesse, and scores of others in Europe, were not about heroes and heroic deeds, but about weeks, months, years in muddy trenches, surrounded with the stench of dying men and dead horses, about barbed wire and poison gas.

In this milieu the American peace movement flourished as organizations multiplied, mastered public relations techniques, and mobilized great masses of ordinary citizens. In the

1920s the peace movement was enormously important in defining the nation's role in world affairs, demanding that officials in Washington reconsider membership in or cooperation with the League of Nations, take the lead in disarmament, join the World Court, and outlaw war. Leaders of peace organizations also led efforts to restrain the more blatant forms of American imperialism. But critical as the work of the peace movement unquestionably was, it is equally clear that the nation's political leaders, certainly men like Hughes and Hoover, had also learned the lessons of the war. The need for American participation in efforts to preserve the peace was widely perceived.

Wilson had recognized that American interests in the world were protected best on two levels: international cooperation and a powerful navy. He understood, as did Hughes, the value of power for obtaining cooperation. The option of League membership appeared closed to Hughes, but there were other approaches available when necessary. One problem that troubled Hughes was pressure to limit naval building at a time when Great Britain and Japan seemed primed to launch new programs utilizing new technology and threatening to return the U.S. Navy to second-class status. The demand for naval disarmament struck administration officials as inopportune, given residual tensions with Japan and the pending renewal of the Anglo-Japanese alliance. Undisputed British primacy on the seas had facilitated previous British interference with American trade. As the American empire expanded, it made little sense to leave it at the mercy of the British Admiralty. Reining in the American navy unilaterally was manifestly not the answer; an international agreement to limit naval building might well be.

Demand that the Harding administration lead the world toward disarmament came from the peace movement and its allies in Congress, especially Senator Borah. In December 1920, Borah introduced a resolution calling for a 50 percent reduction in naval building and a conference with Britain and Japan to preclude an arms race. Initially the Harding administration, toward which the resolution was directed, resisted. Hughes was determined to regain for the executive branch the power over foreign policy which the Senate appeared to have seized in the fight over ratification of the Treaty of Versailles.

In the months before the Senate considered the Borah resolution, before Hughes and Harding had to respond, the peace movement slowly mobilized. Disarmament was an issue of enormous appeal to the movement and the public generally. It was easily understood: Armaments were used for war; therefore, a reduction in armaments reduced the likelihood of war. On another level, theorists argued that war was caused by arms races. If nations could agree to avoid arms races, they could avoid war. Disarmament as a cause also had the virtue of circumventing the fissures within the peace movement. Individuals and groups that had found themselves opposed on the question of American membership in the League of Nations, or on the use of sanctions in world affairs, might unite to stave off an arms race. Even Borah and Senator Hiram Johnson (R–Calif.), leading "irreconcilables" in the fight over ratification of the Treaty of Versailles, were willing to work for an international conference on arms limitation. Hardheaded businessmen could be attracted to the cause by the promise of tax cuts made possible by reduced government spending on armaments. And to men like Hoover and Lamont, disarmament seemed a wonderful way to relieve pressure on government budgets, to free resources for more productive investment at home and abroad.

The single most effective figure in the disarmament cause was Frederick J. Libby, an ordained Congregational minister whose speaking tour in the winter and spring of 1920–1921 helped focus attention on the Borah resolution and spawned petitions, postcards, and telegrams to Congress and the administration. The Federal Council of Churches of Christ, the Women's International League for Peace and Freedom, and the newly formed National League of Women Voters committed their organizational skills to generating support for the resolution. With suffrage won, many women activists concentrated their energies on a variety of efforts to keep the peace.

In May 1921, despite administration objections, the Borah resolution passed the Senate by a vote of 74 to 0. A month later, the House endorsed it overwhelmingly, 332 to 4. Harding and Hughes capitulated and invited Britain and Japan to a conference to discuss arms limitation. The peace movement had demonstrated its power, and Libby moved quickly to increase its effectiveness. In September he organized the National Council for the Limitation of Armaments, a clearing-house for all organizations interested in the cause. Farm organizations and labor organizations, women's groups, representatives of Catholic, Jewish, and Protestant organizations, the Parent-Teachers Association and the National Education Association, as well as various peace societies, joined in the effort. Libby was chosen executive secretary to direct the day-to-day activities of the council. He set up his office in Washington, a few blocks from the site of the pending conference, and immediately created a stunningly impressive educational and lobbying apparatus. The outcome of the conference would not be left to chance—or to government bureaucrats less committed to disarmament than he believed the American people to be.

In London, the British government faced similar public pressure for disarmament, led by labor and women's organizations. The people of Great Britain had suffered infinitely more from the world war, and the cries for an enduring peace could not be ignored. But Prime Minister David Lloyd George had competing pressures to confront. The admirals constituted a far more potent force in British politics than in American, and they were not ready to yield supremacy to their upstart cousins across the Atlantic. Nonetheless, Lloyd George realized that the British economy could not easily sustain an arms race with the United States. Moreover, his cabinet deemed American goodwill an important foreign policy objective. The prime minister had another international political problem which appeared relevant: the question of whether to renew the Anglo-Japanese alliance, due to expire in July 1921 and much disliked by Americans and Canadians.

When the American initiative for an arms limitation conference arrived, the British Foreign Office suggested enlarging the conference to include all nations with interests in East Asia. The importance of navies was unquestionably related to Japanese-American tensions and questions of China. Without a political settlement of East Asian issues, it would be difficult to obtain agreement on arms limitation. Such a settlement might well preempt an arms race and produce a multilateral agreement to replace the Anglo-Japanese alliance. Carefully analyzing the domestic political situation, including grave complications like his need to avoid alienating potential supporters of his Irish policy, Lloyd George concluded his interests lay with naval arms limitation.

Hughes had no difficulty comprehending the value of a larger conference. The United States quickly agreed to issue invitations to Belgium, China, France, Italy, the Netherlands, and Portugal—all nations with interests in the region except Soviet Russia. Here was an opportunity for Warren Harding's America to lead the effort to create an enduring peace, resolve its tensions with Japan, rid the world of the noxious Anglo-Japanese alliance, and obtain international endorsement of its policies in East Asia—an opportunity to preserve the peace, protect the empire, and win widespread domestic approval.

The Japanese government, on the other hand, was very uneasy about accepting the invitation, especially after the initial overture was modified to include issues other than arms limitation. Japanese leaders feared that the United States would use the conference as an international tribunal before which it would attack Japanese imperialism in China and challenge the Anglo-Japanese alliance. The foreign minister, Shidehara Kijuro, asked for and received assurances from Hughes that the matters would not be raised at the conference. But on these issues and the matter of naval arms limitation, Shidehara, Prime Minister Hara Kei, and a wide spectrum of Japanese intellectuals were in fact quite close to the mainstream of Anglo-American thought.

Hara was determined to assert civilian control over the Japanese military. He and Shidehara and many Japanese opinion leaders had been embarrassed by the excesses of Japanese imperialism in China and were eager to demonstrate that Japan was prepared to accept Woodrow Wilson's new world order. Opposition to defense spending had suddenly become politically significant in Japan. The Japanese army, long the dominant force in Japanese politics, was opposed to arms limitation, civilian control, and Wilsonian conceptions of how to deal with China. Naval leaders, however, despite an ambitious and funded building program, recognized that an international agreement to limit naval building might work to

Japan's advantage. They also saw acquiescence as a way to work through Hara to undermine the power of the army. Ultimately a civilian-navy alliance prevailed, and the Japanese delegation left for Washington prepared to reach agreement with the United States and Great Britain.

The enlargement of the conference agenda was a source of great excitement in another nation, whose navy was not deemed much of a threat to anybody. In China, extravagant hopes were raised of using the conference to reverse the failure of Chinese diplomacy at Versailles. The Chinese, despite internal dissension tantamount to civil war, imagined an opportunity to drive Japan out of Shantung and to get all the powers to surrender their special privileges in China—nearly a century of infringements on Chinese sovereignty. They dreamed of tariff autonomy, of an end to extraterritoriality, the elimination of spheres of influence, the removal of foreign troops from Chinese soil and of foreign gunboats from Chinese waters. They had few illusions about their ability to win in any diplomatic confrontation with Japan, but they had many illusions about what they might accomplish with the help of the United States.

The conference opened on 12 November 1921, and Hughes almost immediately shattered the complacency of jaded diplomats and journalists from around the world. Instead of restricting himself to the usual platitudes of welcome, he quickly presented a detailed plan to limit the battle fleet of each of the major naval powers, naming specific ships to be scrapped. He sank more British battleships, remarked one commentator, than all the world's admirals had succeeded in sinking in the history of the British navy. Hughes's approach was magnificent political theater: He gained the attention of the world, and he delighted the peace movement, at home and abroad. The United States had struck a great blow for world peace. But Hughes was not merely performing for the public. His proposals were brilliantly conceived, and he and his staff were ready and able for the extraordinarily complex diplomacy that would be necessary for success.

Before the United States or its rivals for naval leadership would agree to limit naval building, let alone decommission existing battleships, each required assurance that its security and the security of its empire would not be compromised. The greatest tensions were between the United States and Japan in the western Pacific. As a precondition for limiting its navy, the United States wanted the abrogation of the Anglo-Japanese alliance. In addition, the American government wanted guarantees of its rights, principally for commercial cable, on the island of Yap, mandated to Japan at Versailles despite Wilson's protest. While the conference sessions and public attention focused on navies and efforts to internationalize American policy toward China, Hughes secretly negotiated an agreement with Japan over Yap and with Great Britain and Japan to eliminate the alliance.

Neither the British government nor the Japanese wanted to give up the alliance. Arthur J. Balfour, leader of the British delegation, quickly concluded that retention of the alliance would prevent naval disarmament—and that Great Britain needed arms limitation and American goodwill more than it needed the alliance. His alternative, approximating a trilateral alliance of the three leading naval powers, was never seriously considered. Shidehara, negotiating for Japan, drafted a treaty which Hughes modified to a nonaggression pact, into which France was invited.

The resulting Four-Power Treaty specifically replaced the Anglo-Japanese alliance and committed the signatories to respect each other's island possessions in the Pacific and to consult in the event of disagreement or outside threat. The treaty was a tribute to Hughes, who had won elimination of the alliance at no cost to the United States. It was also evidence of the value both Great Britain and Japan placed on American goodwill—and of their awareness that they had to offer concessions to prevent an arms race in which they could not long compete with American wealth.

Nonetheless, the Four-Power Treaty was not popular in the United States. In the Senate and in the streets there was considerable suspicion of the secrecy surrounding the negotiation. Unable or unwilling to comprehend that the treaty was an integral part of the larger arms and Pacific settlements reached at the conference, some senators feared it was a gratuitous entanglement in international politics which, like League membership, would draw the United States involuntarily into war. Careful preparation by Hughes, assisted by the president and key senators, won a narrow 67 to 27 victory for ratification, only 5 votes more than the required two-thirds majority.

The naval arms limitation, or Five-Power Treaty, was enormously pleasing to Libby and the peace movements around the world—and rightly so. For the first time in recorded history, the Great Powers voluntarily surrendered their freedom to arm as they pleased. In Great Britain, Japan, and the United States, internal political considerations facilitated agreement. The leading student of the treaty, Roger Dingman, explains that in the United States, "the politics of domestic leadership demanded American initiatives for arms control and profoundly influenced the character of American proposals for disarmament."[1] In short, the efforts of the peace movement and Harding's unwillingness to lead the United States into the League of Nations forced the administration to turn to naval limitations, an assertion of American leadership for peace of which even Senators Borah and Johnson were supportive.

The Five-Power Treaty negotiators focused on and restricted tonnage in capital ships—battleships and battlecruisers. The treaty contained the name of every ship retained or sacrificed and a schedule of replacements through 1942. Great Britain agreed to rough equality with the United States. Japan, with but one ocean in which to defend its empire, accepted inferiority to both. The ratio of tonnage allowed to the three major naval powers was 5:5:3. The other two powers, France and Italy, accepted ratios of 1:67. Aircraft carriers, whose potential importance was suspected, were also restricted, but the numbers of cruisers, destroyers, and submarines were not. Only the size and offensive power of cruisers were limited. France was primarily responsible for the failure to reach agreement on the smaller ships.

In addition, a clause without which arms control efforts might not have succeeded provided that Great Britain, Japan, and the United States would not build new bases or further fortify existing bases on most of the islands they controlled in the Pacific. For the United States, the agreement covered the Aleutians, Midway, Wake, Tutuila, Guam, and the Philippines. For Japan, it included the Kuriles, Bonins, Ryukyus, Formosa, and the Pescadores. For Great Britain, it included all island possessions except Singapore, Australia, New Zealand, and Canadian offshore islands. In effect, the nonfortification agreement and the limits on naval building left Japan dominant in the western Pacific and the United States secure in the eastern Pacific and western Atlantic. The British reigned supreme from their home waters to the Straits of Malacca.

Gaps in the agreement relating to small ships and the absence of once major naval powers Germany and Russia were among the flaws of the Five-Power Treaty, but its signing constituted a most important historic moment, filled with promise for all who wished to be spared future war. Japanese-American tensions over Yap, naval bases, and naval threats eased markedly, and the two countries had new evidence that they could negotiate their differences. It established the basis for further cooperation, and an era of good feeling between the two nations. All Hughes surrendered were ships and bases for which Congress was unlikely to appropriate essential funds. Again, the Harding administration was rightfully proud of its diplomacy and deserving of its public relations success.

The third major agreement to come out of the conference was the Nine-Power Treaty relating to China. The primary purpose of the treaty was to stabilize the competition among the powers to preclude rivalry in China from erupting in war. To this end, the powers agreed not to meddle in China's internal affairs and not to seek new privileges at Chinese expense. In words Americans had urged so many times before, all agreed to respect the "sovereignty, the independence, territorial and administrative integrity of China" and to attempt to establish the principle of equal opportunity for the commerce and industry of all in China.

The Chinese quest for tangible concessions toward the elimination of existing imperialist privileges was considered outside the conference and generally brushed aside. Of greatest importance were Japanese-Chinese negotiations in which Balfour advised the Japanese and Hughes and members of his staff advised the Chinese, sitting in on a total of thirty-six sessions. Japan finally agreed to return the leasehold it had seized in Shantung, while retaining important railway privileges for another fifteen years. The Chinese struggle for tariff autonomy and an end to extraterritoriality failed, however. A customs convention was signed which threw the Chinese a few crumbs, in the form of a 5 percent increase in duties, but French obstruction turned even that into less than it appeared. All China could get was a promise to investigate tariff and judicial questions—and that came to naught in the years that followed. The response in China and among Chinese students in the United States was angry. Among Americans, however, the signing of the Nine-Power Treaty satisfied the desire to do something for the heathen Chinese and there was great satisfaction at international acceptance of the American formula.

The Washington Conference of 1921–1922 was an extraordinary event, symbolic of America's new role in world affairs. An international conference of tremendous importance was held in the United States, largely at American initiative, organized by the United States, and dominated by its secretary of state. As great powers are wont to do, the United States broke Japan's diplomatic code, intercepted messages between Tokyo and the Japanese delegation, and knew just how far to push. Every important American objective was achieved: arms control, abrogation of the Anglo-Japanese alliance, a limit on imperialism in China, protection of American rights in China and on Yap. Peace and the empire would be preserved without putting the lives of American boys at risk. None of the agreements reached at the conference required the United States to use force or committed the United States to any action other than to consult with the others in any crisis.

The Washington Conference was also a triumph for Wilson's vision of a new world order. Great Britain, Japan, and the United States would cooperate in peaceful rivalry without further harm to weaker countries like China. The Pacific treaty system, designed primarily by Hughes and his staff but understood and accepted by Balfour and Shidehara, envisaged a cooperative system for East Asia—a system in which none of the powers would attempt to maximize its advantage. Once assured that the Americans were not threatening their "special interests" in Manchuria and Inner Mongolia, the Japanese were quite willing, even eager, to adopt the system. Japanese-American friendship bloomed—only to be undermined by the racist legislative action of 1924 excluding Japanese immigrants. Nonetheless, the Pacific system endured until it was shattered by an unexpected force: the Chinese revolution (see Chapter 4).

II

After the exhilaration of the Washington Conference's successes faded, public interest in the peace movement and world affairs naturally declined. Some Americans doubtless believed that the conference had solved all the world's problems —certainly those pertinent to the United States—and secure in that belief, returned to the usual preoccupations with making money. For distractions there were opportunities to swallow goldfish, sit on flagpoles, or ogle flappers—or whatever the new morals and manners of postwar society might permit. Within the peace movement, however, there was general awareness that the foundation of an enduring peace was not yet complete. Further disarmament was necessary. There remained strong interest in world organizations, both the League and the World Court, and there was growing support for the idea of outlawing war. At the core of the American peace movement were fewer than a hundred full-time workers determined to maintain a high level of public interest and to keep official Washington actively involved in strengthening the world's peace machinery.

The Harding administration had kept the League of Nations at arm's length throughout 1921, sometimes quite rudely. The president had decided that the issue was settled: The United States would neither join with nor cooperate with the League. The League was dead and, for a while, correspondence from League officials was placed unanswered in the Department of State's dead letter file. When the League survived American rejection, Harding and others were willing to credit it with being useful for Europe, but unnecessary for the United States. Even the Democratic party came to see the League issue as a liability by 1924, and Wilsonian loyalists failed to get the platform committee to promise to seek membership for the United States.

Within the peace movement, however, efforts to gain membership or at least align the United States with the League persisted for some time with considerable success. Especially after the favorable outcome of the Washington Conference, Hughes seemed more responsive to the League. It was clear to administration leaders that Congress and the American public welcomed international cooperation that did not threaten to embroil the United States in foreign wars. Much of the credit for creating a climate of opinion conducive to working with the League must go to the peace movement. Organizations like Libby's, in 1922 renamed the National Council for the Prevention of War, maintained a constant campaign to generate grassroots support and to lobby Congress. Libby was a master of all of the necessary activities. He continued his very successful speaking tours, stimulating petition drives, letters, and telegrams to public officials everywhere he went. He and his staff prepared and planted releases in small-town newspapers all over the country. They wrote speeches for congressmen. They were exceptionally good at mustering farm and labor support. In good years, Libby was able to raise a budget of well over $100,000, most of it in very small contributions. In the 1920s, a frugal lobbyist could work miracles with a budget of that size.

Working toward a similar end, men like Nicholas Murray Butler, James T. Shotwell, and Clark Eichelberger lobbied at the highest levels of government. Persuaded that public and congressional pressures on the executive were more often than not counterproductive, Butler, a Republican presidential hopeful as well as president of Columbia University and the Carnegie Endowment for Peace, talked and wrote to his good friend, Charles Evans Hughes. Shotwell, a Columbia professor and director of the Carnegie Endowment, had ready access to the senior members of Hughes's staff. Eichelberger, who headed the Chicago office of the League of Nations Non-Partisan Association (later League of Nations Association), could assure the secretary of state of the support of opinion leaders outside New York. Though they differed on tactics and in their respective conceptions of the League as well, men like Libby and Butler complemented each other well as they neutralized public, congressional, and bureaucratic opposition to working with the League.

After the Washington Conference, League officials and American diplomats corresponded formally and met informally to discuss all the major issues of world politics. The United States posted a series of its ablest diplomats—Joseph C. Grew, Hugh Gibson, and Hugh Wilson—to Switzerland, where they looked after American interests at League headquarters in Geneva as well as the modest demands at the Swiss capital in Berne. Unofficial observers represented the United States at League meetings, and by 1925 Grew attended as the official representative of his government. From 1925 onward there was an American official present at every League conference dealing with arms control and at most conferences dealing with economic and social issues. Moreover, the American government signed several treaties and conventions that derived from these meetings.

League officials were heartened by the American presence and encouraged by conversations with the pro-League American leaders with whom they were most likely to have contact. The dream of American membership died hard on both sides of the Atlantic. The United States never sought membership, and no administration was willing to commit itself to support the League to the extent that League officials and supporters thought essential if the League was to function effectively. Nonetheless, sustained American participation in League affairs far surpassed the prewar level of involvement in international affairs and the expectations of those who had witnessed the apparent rejection of the League by the Senate in 1919 and 1920 and by the Harding administration in 1921.

A substantial minority of Americans appears to have had serious objections to the League in the 1920s, some viewing it as an instrument of British and French imperialism, and others fearing League Covenant provisions for collective security would enmesh the United States in wars of someone else's choosing. On the other hand, there was widespread, nearly unanimous support for membership in the World Court. Hughes and Harding, Calvin Coolidge and his secretary of state, Frank B. Kellogg, Hoover and his secretary, Henry L. Stimson, all favored joining the Court—as did the majority of congressmen and senators. Poor diplomacy and dilatory handling at critical moments prevented consummation of the necessary arrangements.

Harding submitted a proposal for the United States to adhere to the Protocol and Statute of the World Court early in 1923, but he died before the Senate acted. In the Senate, Lodge and Borah, consecutive chairmen of the Committee on Foreign Relations, kept the proposal from reaching the floor. Both men were hostile to the World Court as a subsidiary of the League, despite Borah's interest in international law as an instrument for maintaining peace. After several efforts by Coolidge and endorsement of membership by both parties in 1924, the House of Representatives approved the idea by a wide margin in March 1925. Finally, in January 1926 the Senate gave its overwhelming approval.

Unfortunately for those who hoped to see the United States join the World Court, Senate approval had been subject to five conditions. The fifth of these, permitting the United States to prevent the Court from giving advisory opinions on matters in which it claimed an interest, met objections from other Court members. Twice the League Council suggested negotiations and twice Coolidge and Kellogg refused. Unable to bluff the council into dropping its objections and unwilling to negotiate, Coolidge dropped the idea. In retrospect, the United States had nothing to lose by negotiating, and the behavior of the American government, demanding privileges other Court members did not share, was reprehensible. On the other hand, if drawing the United States closer to the League was a paramount concern of League members and officials, then perhaps yielding a bit more to appease the Americans was in order.

In the United States, peace movement leaders were outraged and continued their efforts to gain membership in the Court. They were able to enlist Hughes and the venerable Republican statesman and father of the foreign policy establishment, Elihu Root, to assist in their efforts. Root eventually went to Geneva, where he was largely responsible for the redesigning of the Court Protocol to meet the conditions posed by the U.S. Senate. In December 1929 the United States signed. Again backers were frustrated, as Hoover gave priority to arms control and the Great Depression overtook Senate consideration until after Franklin Roosevelt was in the White House. The United States never became a member of the World Court.

III

One other cause in which the peace movement united was the quest for the outlawing of war. Ultimately, the efforts of peace activists and the aims of French Foreign Minister Aristide Briand overlapped and led to the Kellogg-Briand or Paris Peace Pact of 1928.

The single most important figure in the outlawry movement was a wealthy Chicago lawyer, Salmon O. Levinson. Levinson was a pacifist, convinced that international law could contain the impulse to war. He argued that if war were made illegal, there would be no more wars. It was necessary to get all nations to agree to such a law, as through a multilateral treaty. Levinson was publicizing the phrase "outlawry of war" even before the battle over ratification of the Treaty of Versailles and American membership in the League. He opposed the League because he objected to the provisions in the Covenant for sanctions and collective security—a potential for the use of force he would not countenance. In 1919 and 1920, however, the League issue engaged the attention of his potential audience. In 1921 and 1922, the peace movement concentrated its energies on arms control. Finally, in 1923, Levinson persuaded Borah to introduce a resolution in the Senate incorporating his program: a call for a universal treaty outlawing war, with each nation responsible for punishing its own warmongers. All disputes would have to be resolved peacefully, by negotiation or arbitration. Despite considerable interest within the peace movement—not least from the great American philosopher John Dewey—no American or foreign political leader took the idea seriously. Levinson wrote hundreds of letters drumming up support and was seconded by the influential *Christian Century,* but several years passed without progress.

The principal catalyst for bringing Levinson's dream to reality was James T. Shotwell, whose goals were quite different. Shotwell was a strong supporter of the League of Nations, eager to draw the United States closer to the League. Shotwell often contended that American cooperation with Great Britain and France was crucial to world peace. United, the democracies could provide international peace and justice. In the spring of 1927, Shotwell met with Briand in Paris in the hope of bringing their two countries closer.

French leaders of the 1920s were intensely fearful for the security of their nation, specifically from attack by Germany. France had been victorious in 1918 only because it had been allied with Russia, Great Britain, Italy, and the United States. French leaders knew that alone they could not prevail against Germany. France had suffered heavy losses during the war, and these were reflected in a very low postwar birth rate. Germany started with a larger population base and had a higher birth rate. French leaders believed that their only hope of surviving that inevitable day when the Germans came seeking revenge was to find allies, to sign pacts with as many nations as possible, alliances if they could be obtained, nonaggression pacts at minimum. It was this pattern of French thinking that Shotwell sought to exploit.

Briand sent an open letter to the American people, drafted by Shotwell, in which the French foreign minister proposed a bilateral treaty to outlaw war. In effect, the agreement was a negative alliance. If the United States signed and France went to war, the United States would not be able to take reprisals against France if the French violated America's neutral rights, as had Great Britain from 1914 to 1917. Briand liked the idea for the same reason Shotwell liked it: If successful, the scheme would involve the United States in the French security system. For Briand such involvement was an end in itself; for Shotwell it was a step toward further collective action by the United States.

Kellogg and Coolidge were irritated by Briand's public diplomacy and by no means interested in becoming involved in the French security system. They had every intention of ignoring the overture, but Shotwell was not without further resources. At his initiative, Nicholas Murray Butler wrote to the *New York Times* calling attention to Briand's letter. The *Times* published Butler's letter and endorsed the Briand proposal. A massive campaign by the peace movement followed. Levinson and Libby mobilized all their resources, but the campaign transcended the efforts of a few individuals. All the peace organizations and their compatriots in church groups, women's organizations, and educational associations joined in. They organized petition drives, letter-writing campaigns, and lobbying visits to Congress and to the secretary of state. Kellogg began receiving more than 300 letters a day and at one point noted that more than 50,000 people had registered their support for Briand's proposal. When an attempt to extend the arms control agreements of 1921–1922 to cruisers failed at Geneva in August 1927, the peace movement redoubled its effort to outlaw war. One petition gathered by the Federal Council of Churches contained 180,000 signatures. Clearly Kellogg and Coolidge had little choice.

The secretary of state and his president wanted no part of Briand's treaty, but they could not ignore the pressures generated by the peace movement. A solution to their dilemma emerged in December 1927. The United States proposed substituting a multilateral treaty to be signed by all nations. In this way the United States could evade Briand's snare and still endorse peace, the outlawing of war. Levinson, Libby, and others enrolled in the campaign were delighted. Every nation would promise not to go to war with every other nation—and the heavenly city would be upon us.

Briand was not pleased by Kellogg's ploy, but there was no escape. The peace movement in Europe was also determined to seize this opportunity and Briand, no more than Kellogg or Coolidge, could not appear to oppose peace. And so, in August 1928, in Paris, the Great Powers signed a pact to which all but a few insignificant countries adhered. Germany, Japan, and Italy, as well as the United States, France, and Great Britain, undertook a solemn obligation to renounce war as an instrument of national policy. Nations and U.S. senators with reservations about fighting in self-defense or under obligations of the League Covenant were heard—and their reservations swept under the rug by Kellogg. Ultimately, sixty-four nations signed the pact. In the U.S. Senate, consent for the treaty was obtained quickly by a vote of 85 to 1. For his efforts, the American secretary of state was awarded the Nobel Prize for Peace.

Few peace movement leaders and perhaps no diplomats or

senators believed that the Kellogg Pact had put an end to war. The American public was generally delighted because the United States had played a leading role in strengthening the "machinery" for world peace. If they could not be certain that war had been eliminated, they believed they had at least made the use of force more difficult to justify. They had improved the odds for peace. The Kellogg Pact and the fact that a Quaker, Herbert Hoover, had been elected to the presidency in 1928, heartened Libby, but he still thought it essential for the United States to join the World Court and the League and to obtain arms reductions around the world. Shotwell and Butler had always had additional collective security measures on their agenda. Similarly, in Europe and on the League Council, the enormous satisfaction with the American role in the pact was predicated on the assumption that the United States would now cooperate still more with the League and accept more and more responsibility for the maintenance of world peace.

The Kellogg Pact confirmed the power of the peace movement as a force in the shaping of American foreign policy. Those within the movement who were eager to have the United States join the League remained frustrated, as did the much larger number who wanted membership for their country on the World Court, but the record of the 1920s was impressive: the first major arms control agreement of modern times and a multilateral treaty to renounce the use of force. Moreover, the peace movement created a milieu in the United States in the 1920s which greatly restricted the freedom of the executive to use American power in "police actions" in the Caribbean and China or to coerce Mexico (see Chapter 4). The strength of the peace movement ensured that the American quest for wealth and power would be pursued peacefully.

Internationally, the United States had established itself as an important pillar of world peace. It was not as cooperative as League officials and French and British diplomats might have liked, but American secretaries of state, Hughes and Kellogg, were the architects of arms control, the Pacific treaty system, and the Kellogg Peace Pact. Rarely had the presence of the United States been so strongly felt in the foreign ministries of the world. The American people were in the forefront of the search for peace and prosperity.

CHAPTER 4

THE RESPONSE TO REVOLUTION AND INSTABILITY

I

As the United States exerted its enormous economic power across the world and its statesmen joined those of other nations to work for an enduring peace, Americans in and out of government were forced to become more concerned about local affairs in distant lands. Instability threatened the world order in which American interests, economic and strategic, prospered. Revolution might destroy that order. In the 1920s, to an unprecedented extent, the United States became involved in efforts to cope with revolution and instability in Russia, China, Mexico, and Germany—as well as in its Caribbean protectorates.

Closest to home was the Mexican Revolution, with which successive governments in Washington had failed to come to terms since the dictatorship of Porfirio Díaz had been overthrown in 1911. At the conclusion of the world war, tension between the United States and Mexico signaled the possibility of renewed armed conflict. Republican party leaders castigated Wilson for failing to protect the lives and property of U.S citizens south of the border. Secretary of State Robert Lansing maneuvered toward a break in relations with Mexico. Others in the United States recalled Mexico's flirtation with Germany in 1916 and 1917. Wilson recovered sufficiently from the stroke he suffered in September 1919 to avert a break or intervention, but the issues raised by the Mexican Revolution were not resolved and tensions persisted as the Harding administration took office.

In November 1920, after months of unrest and the assassination of Wilson's old antagonist, Venustiano Carranza, Alvaro Obregón was elected president of Mexico. In the contemporaneous election campaign in the United States, both major parties pledged to withhold recognition of a new Mexican government until agreement was reached on the claims of American citizens against Mexico. The outgoing Wilson administration did not extend recognition to Obregón.

Central to the dispute between the two countries was Article 27 of the Mexican Constitution of 1917, through which Mexico tried to reclaim land and resources sold to foreigners by Díaz. Specifically, Article 27 claimed that the land and subsoil rights of Mexico belonged to the Mexican people—at a time when more than 40 percent of the land and 60 percent of the oil industry was owned and controlled by citizens of the United States. Americans who had invested in Mexican lands were outraged by the threat to their investments, and the major oil companies could not tolerate a confiscatory policy that might be imitated by other underdeveloped countries. In addition, the Mexican constitution provided what the historian Charles C. Cumberland called the "most enlightened statement of labor protective principles in the world to that date,"[1] perceived by American businessmen as a threat to their profits and the control of their enterprises in Mexico.

The Mexican government, challenging existing interpretations of international law and contracts, asserted the right of its people to their patrimony. The government of the United States supported the claims of its citizens. It was not a question of right and wrong, but of conflicting rights. Historically, conflicts of this sort are resolved in favor of the contestant able to muster superior force. In this instance, a weak nation was challenging its powerful neighbor—the very country which had emerged from the war as the most powerful nation in the world and which had demonstrated its willingness to use force against Mexico on several previous occasions. The odds for the achievement of Mexican aspirations were not good.

Harding and Hughes continued the policy of withholding recognition from the Obregón administration, a strategy which was not without effect. Obregón wanted recognition for the legitimacy it would bestow at home and abroad. Of greater importance was the fact that it would be extremely difficult to borrow needed capital from foreign investors without recognition. Borrowing in the absence of recognition by the United States was particularly difficult in the 1920s, when American investors were the only ones with capital to spare. Obregón was willing to give Harding and Hughes verbal assurances that his government would not enforce Article 27 stringently. They would not accept anything less than a treaty. Obregón could not offer a treaty if he hoped to retain power and some semblance of control over the revolution. There was no progress in 1921, no recognition, and no loan.

Prorecognition sentiment increased in the United States among businessmen eager to export goods to Mexico and even among the smaller oil companies more afraid of the giants in their own industry than of Mexican revolutionaries. Hughes was unyielding, depending for advice on Mexican affairs on Henry P. Fletcher, his undersecretary, and Matthew E. Hanna, chief of the Division of Mexican Affairs—both of whom had served under Wilson and were persuaded he had not been tough enough. Indeed, Fletcher had resigned as ambassador to Mexico when Wilson refused to increase pressure on Carranza. Fletcher and Hanna insisted that Obregón could not be trusted and that even if he could be, he could not deliver on his promise. The impasse continued on into 1922.

At this point, Thomas Lamont came to the rescue. Lamont's principal concern was the collection of Mexico's debt to American bondholders. Settlement of the debt question was improbable without a political settlement and the bondholders, unlike the oilmen and the mining interests, were indifferent to Article 27 and favored recognition. Nor did the bondholders worry at all about new taxes on American oil companies in Mexico when the income could be used by the Mexican government to pay off its debts. Lamont, as was so often the case in the 1920s, emerged as the leader of an International Committee of Bankers seeking to collect from Mexico. Deftly, he persuaded British bankers not to take advantage of American bankers' unwillingness to lend to Mexico: Anglo-American bankers presented a united front. A settlement of old debts would have to precede new loans.

Lamont kept his friend Charles Evans Hughes informed of his activities and worked with Hughes's advisers to coordinate with government ends—insofar as they did not jeopardize his purposes.

Obregón wanted a new development loan which only Lamont could deliver. In June 1922 he directed his negotiator, Adolfo De la Huerta, to sign an agreement with Lamont. The Lamont–De la Huerta agreement contained a Mexican commitment to pay the full service on its debt after five years, in return for which Lamont was willing to waive overdue interest and acquiesce in the Mexican export tax on oil which the oilmen rather than the bankers would have to pay. There was no agreement on a new loan.

Brushing aside the outrage of the National Association for Protection of American Rights in Mexico and the American Association of Mexico (led by William Buckley, father of the Reagan era conservative columnist) demanding intervention against alleged Bolsheviks in Mexico, Lamont persuaded Hughes that Obregón was a man with whom the United States could deal. Hanna, handling Mexican affairs at the middle level of the Department of State, also was persuaded that Obregón had demonstrated reasonableness and durability. With Lamont as broker, the United States and Mexico agreed to hold bilateral talks in 1923. At the Bucareli Conference, the two sides reached a modus vivendi. The United States surrendered its insistence on a treaty and accepted the Doctrine of Positive Acts, an interpretation of Article 27 by the Mexican courts which excluded land which had been developed prior to the coming into force of the Constitution from its provision. The Mexicans compromised further by agreeing to provide compensation (in bonds rather than cash) for expropriated properties up to 1,775 hectares. Shortly thereafter, the new American president, Calvin Coolidge, extended recognition to the Obregón government. The crisis was over—although the oilmen remained angry and even Lamont, the hero of the story, was irritated by Mexico's subsequent inability to meet the repayment schedule as promised.

As usual in world affairs, the 1923 settlement between Mexico and the United States did not prove to be a permanent solution. A year later, Obregón's presidency ended and he was succeeded by Plutarco Elías Calles. Buckley and his cohorts renewed their cries of Bolshevism, and Calles provided grist for their mill with attacks on the Catholic Church and a new law limiting to fifty years possession of oil lands acquired before 1917. And once again J. P. Morgan and Company rode to the rescue.

Part of the problem was the American ambassador, James R. Sheffield, who, like so many diplomats, found his closest associates among the local aristocrats and shared their hostility to the revolution—and their contempt for Calles and the other "Indians." Sheffield was also responsive to demands of American oil companies and other Yankee capitalists whose interests were threatened by Calles's reforms. The new Secretary of State, Frank B. Kellogg, put his trust in Sheffield and declared that Mexico was on trial before the world. He challenged the Mexicans to fulfill their international obligations, specifically the Bucareli agreements. When Calles and the Mexican legislature disregarded warnings from Sheffield and Kellogg, calls for intervention resounded in Washington.

Throughout 1926, the threat of war between the United States and Mexico grew. Complicating relations was the situation in Nicaragua, where the United States was having trouble extricating itself from its protectorate (see below). Kellogg's staff perceived a Mexican plot to dominate Central America by backing the Nicaraguan rebels against the Washington-backed regime. The Mexicans, they argued, were trying to spread Bolshevism, and it was time to send in the U.S. Marines. The Marines landed in Nicaragua in December 1926 and Assistant Secretary of State Robert E. Olds orchestrated a campaign to prepare the American people for the use of force, if necessary, against Mexico. To a skeptical press, Olds outlined the justification for U.S. action in Central America. Kellogg followed in January 1927 by arguing before the Senate Committee on Foreign Relations that Russian agents had been active in Mexico and the Bolsheviks were attempting to undermine American influence in the region.

Few Americans maintained good contacts with the Calles government. Foremost among them was Lamont who, in December 1925, had succeeded in negotiating another debt settlement (the Lamont–Pani agreement) with Mexico. He and his partners lobbied vigorously with Coolidge and Kellogg, but Lamont had yet to win Kellogg's confidence. The Minnesota politician had never been comfortable with the Eastern establishment. As the war scare intensified, however, Lamont found formidable allies in the press, the unions, the peace movement, and the Senate. With Frederick Libby leading, the NCPW and the Federal Council of Churches of Christ in America mobilized public opinion against war with Mexico. In the Senate, Kellogg's prattle about Bolshevism was ridiculed. Unanimously, the Senate called for arbitration, for the peaceful solution of differences between Mexico and the United States.

Coolidge and Kellogg were forced to retreat. Lamont persuaded the president that a mutually beneficial agreement could be reached with Mexico, and Coolidge made the requisite conciliatory gestures in April. Lamont offered and Coolidge appointed another Morgan partner (and college friend of the president), Dwight Morrow, as ambassador to Mexico.

Morrow proved to be an extraordinarily good choice. He was exceptionally sensitive to Mexican aspirations and to the political requirements of Calles. Morrow and Calles developed an excellent personal relationship. Morrow's style, especially when contrasted with that of his predecessor, won friends and eased tensions. He arranged two successful goodwill tours, the first by his son-in-law, the heroic and worldpopular aviator Charles Lindbergh, and the second by the humorist Will Rogers. In his hands, substantive issues disappeared almost as easily.

The central problem was still Article 27 of the Mexican Constitution. The American oil companies demanded a complete and permanent guarantee of all their holdings in Mexico. Calles—and all other Mexican leaders—were committed to nationalization of subsoil rights. Threats were not likely to be productive, and the government of the United States refrained from any. On the other hand, Morrow persuaded Calles that an intractable stand contrary to what industrial creditor nations considered international law would hurt Mexico, would preclude the possibility of obtaining development loans. Calles would have to settle for a more gradualist, reformist approach. He would have to return to Obregón's doctrine of positive acts. Morrow pointed to a case pending in the Mexican courts that could be used to that end—and lo, the court reaffirmed the doctrine of positive acts. Calles then directed the legislature to amend the law to conform with the court ruling, and the problem disappeared. In March 1928, the U.S. Department of State announced that differences between the United States and Mexico no longer existed. The oil companies were not satisfied, but were denied the support from Washington they demanded. Even the oil companies, however, had avoided what Morrow knew they feared most: a precedent for unqualified nationalization of subsoil rights without compensation.

Morrow also helped Calles out of the mess into which the Mexican president's anticlericalism had gotten him. For three years the Mexican bishops had refused to say Mass and the Cristeros, supporters of the Church, were in armed rebellion. In the United States, publicists for the Catholic Church were among the leaders of those calling for intervention. Buckley was in the happy position of being able to fight simultaneously for his God and his profits. Morrow imported an American Catholic priest, John Burke, who was sympathetic to Calles's reforms and mediated between Calles and the Mexican bishops. Church affairs took a little longer to resolve than economic affairs, but by mid-1929 Morrow's efforts were blessed with a settlement: Mass could be heard again in Mexico and the Cristeros faded away.

Morrow's diplomacy was enormously successful. In an era in which public support for intervention had evaporated, in which gunboat diplomacy was anathema to the public and its elected representatives in Congress, diplomacy had to be cultivated. Lamont and Morrow, even when they worked at cross purposes, as was often the case when Lamont's concern for bondholder interests and Morrow's efforts to help Calles reorganize Mexican finances conflicted, served their country well. Friendly relations with Mexico were reestablished without sacrificing any important interest. Here was one thread woven into the mantle of Good Neighbor with which the United States sought to wrap its affairs with Latin America by the end of the 1920s.

The postwar milieu in which the Harding and Coolidge

administrations addressed tensions arising out of the Mexican Revolution also affected the way in which the United States coped with its empire in the Caribbean. Anti-imperialist sentiment was strong among the intellectuals and among Americans caught up in the peace movement. The call for self-determination in Wilson's Fourteen Points tapped a spring of sentiment never far from the surface in American attitudes toward world affairs. If self-determination was good for former subjects of the Austrian, Ottoman, and Russian empires, why not for the peoples of Latin America? Countless books and articles critical of American imperialism in the Caribbean began to appear. Prewar muckraking techniques, so successful in bringing about domestic reforms, were applied to foreign policy issues. A public unwilling to countenance the use of force in world affairs was apprised of the activities of American Marines in the Dominican Republic, Haiti, and Nicaragua. As the influence of American business in Latin America grew, the American public was warned of the dangers of the flag following the dollar, of the marines protecting American investments. And in Congress there was considerable irritation, expressed most vehemently by Borah, at the cost of the empire and at what congressmen perceived as executive usurpation of their constitutional right to declare war whenever the president sent in the marines.

There had to be a change in American policy, given the prevailing climate of opinion. The Republican party recognized political reality in the campaign of 1920 by criticizing Wilson's occupation of the Dominican Republic and calling for the withdrawal of American forces from that benighted country. Moreover, the security concerns with which some American leaders had earlier justified "protectorates" in the Caribbean had vanished with the defeat of Germany in the world war. Businessmen were divided on this as on most foreign policy issues. There was no imperative for keeping American forces in place, and many good reasons for getting out. Hughes came to Washington in 1921 with a plan to withdraw from the Dominican Republic and the hope of reducing the American military presence in the Caribbean.

Hughes and most other American leaders still viewed the Caribbean, of necessity, as an American lake. The United

Hegemony in the Caribbean

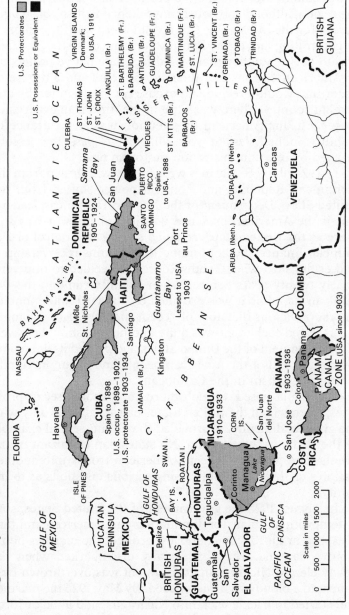

U.S. Protectorates

U.S. Possessions or Equivalent

FLORIDA

GULF OF MEXICO

YUCATAN PENINSULA

MEXICO

BRITISH HONDURAS

Belize

GUATEMALA

Guatemala

San Salvador

EL SALVADOR

HONDURAS

Tegucigalpa

GULF OF HONDURAS

BAY IS.

ROATAN I.

SWAN I.

GULF OF FONSECA

PACIFIC OCEAN

NICARAGUA
1910–1933

Managua
Lake Nicaragua

Corinto

San Jose

CORN IS.

San Juan del Norte

San Juan del Norte

COSTA RICA

PANAMA
1903–1936

Colon

Panama

PANAMA CANAL ZONE (USA since 1903)

COLOMBIA

ISLE OF PINES

Havana

CUBA
Spain to 1898
U.S. occup., 1898–1902
U.S. protectorate 1903–1934

Santiago

JAMAICA (Br.)

Kingston

CARIBBEAN SEA

Guantanamo
Bay
Leased to USA
1903

Môle
St. Nicholas

HAITI

Port au Prince

Samana
Bay

San Juan

DOMINICAN REPUBLIC
1905–1924

SANTO DOMINGO

BAHAMAS (Br.)

NASSAU

ATLANTIC OCEAN

PUERTO RICO
Spain;
to USA, 1898

CULEBRA

ST. THOMAS
ST. JOHN
ST. CROIX

VIEQUES

VIRGIN ISLANDS
Denmark;
to USA, 1916

ANGUILLA (Br.)

ST. BARTHELEMY (Fr.)

BARBUDA (Br.)

ANTIGUA (Br.)

GUADELOUPE (Fr.)

DOMINICA (Br.)

MARTINIQUE (Fr.)

ST. LUCIA (Br.)

ST. VINCENT (Br.)

GRENADA (Br.)

TOBAGO (Br.)

TRINIDAD (Br.)

LESSER ANTILLES

ST. KITTS (Br.)

BARBADOS (Br.)

CURAÇAO (Neth.)

ARUBA (Neth.)

Caracas

VENEZUELA

BRITISH GUIANA

Scale in miles

0 500 1000 1500 2000

States could never tolerate the presence of another power in the region, although obviously a weakened British role would persist for the foreseeable future. But there was little interest in controlling any of the Latin American countries. The task was to devise a policy that would facilitate native protection of American citizens and their investments and a degree of order that would preclude an excuse for intervention by any foreign country. There was little in the American experience to suggest that American intervention was an assurance of stability; nonetheless it was difficult to pass the lessons learned by one administration on to the next.

In 1924, the U.S. Marines were finally withdrawn from the Dominican Republic, and political power shifted from the United States Department of the Navy to Dominican leaders. But if the American presence was less obvious, it was still there as the United States retained significant control of Dominican finances by continuing the customs receivership it had established when Teddy Roosevelt decided to intervene nearly twenty years before. When stability came to the Dominican Republic it was provided by Rafael Trujillo, one of the more vicious dictators of recent memory. How Dominicans treated each other was quite another question, however. The government of the United States had proved itself responsive to the will of the American people and begun its retreat from imperialism in the Caribbean.

Nicaragua posed a much more complicated set of problems, from which the United States extracted itself only with the greatest difficulty. It provided the quintessential example of the perils of intervention. No statesman cognizant of the events there would ever send American troops into another nation's civil war without raising serious questions as to his sanity.

In August 1925 the government of the United States, consistent with its plan for liquidating the American military presence in Caribbean countries, brought the marines home from Nicaragua. They had hardly disembarked when the newly elected Nicaraguan government was overthrown by a coup and a bloody civil war ensued. By May 1926 the marines had started to trickle back into Nicaragua, and a major force was landed in December. Mexico, considered by some American officials to be an agent of Soviet Russia in the New World, supported one side and the United States the other. Apprehensive of the administration's intentions, fearful of a major war in Central America, perhaps even an invasion of Mexico, public opposition mounted. Despite tough words by President Coolidge, it was clear that the support necessary to sustain military intervention did not exist in the United States. The president called upon Henry L. Stimson, a lawyer with a distinguished career in public service, to devise a settlement in Nicaragua.

The United States could not impose upon Nicaragua a government of American choice. To attempt to do so would have required the U.S. Marines to destroy opposition forces and to remain in Nicaragua as an army of occupation. It would have meant mounting American casualties, a price few Americans were willing to pay to maintain the empire. The United States might abandon the Nicaraguan political leaders they preferred and let Nicaraguan civil strife be resolved by Nicaraguans. That course, however sensible, was deemed inconceivable in Washington—in large part because of Mexican support for the opposition and fear of surrendering American influence in Central America. Stimson therefore had to find a way to end the civil strife and bring into existence a government satisfactory to the United States, able to sustain itself and protect American interests, without the presence of U.S. Marines.

Stimson quickly concluded that past American policy had failed, that in the absence of free elections Nicaraguans opposed to the existing government could effect change only through revolution, which the United States tried to prevent. As soon as the U.S. forces left, the revolutionary cycle would begin anew. Stimson based his approach on educating the Nicaraguans to appreciate the value of free elections. The U.S. Marines would maintain order only until a local constabulary could be trained to take over.

The task of preparing and supervising Nicaraguan elections proved horrendous, requiring large numbers of American administrators and military personnel to involve themselves in a wide range of complex local affairs. The mission was costly and unpopular in the United States. Although elections supervised by the United States in 1928, 1930, and 1932 were considered fair by both major parties, because of a split within the Liberal party, internal peace did not come. One Liberal general, Anastasio Somoza, became commander of the constabulary, the Guardia Nacional. Another, César Augusto Sandino, refused to accept the agreement Stimson negotiated in 1928, took to the hills with his men, and vowed to rid Nicaragua of Yankee invaders. Somoza became the hated dictator whose family maintained order in Nicaragua for more than forty years. Sandino, an American-killing bandit to the U.S. government, became a folk hero not only in Nicaragua, but in much of Latin America, his legend enhanced by his ultimate betrayal and murder at Somoza's direction. The U.S. Marines, who chased him for years, came close enough to be ambushed, but their quarry always slipped away. It was January 1933 before the last of the marines came home.

Stimson, to be sure, learned a valuable lesson, which he took with him to Washington when he became secretary of state in the Hoover administration. It was relatively easy to involve American forces in the civil strife of another country —and virtually impossible to create in that other country conditions under which the troops could be withdrawn with a sense of mission accomplished. American ideas about the value of free elections for Nicaragua or any other country were doubtless salutary, but if important sectors in the other country chose other means, the price of imposing the American solution was much too high. Never again—at least not for anyone aware of the American experience in Nicaragua in the 1920s.

That experience in Nicaragua reinforced the reluctance of the United States to use force anywhere in the empire, even in Latin America, where the public historically had been less skittish. There were few places left where 100 U.S. Marines could pacify the populace without incurring casualties or requiring reinforcements. An aroused public, quickly mobilized by the organized peace movement, would not tolerate presidential warmaking. The dominion of the United States in the

Caribbean would have to be sustained by persuasion, by political means, by diplomacy.

The American government was not willing to deny itself the right to intervene in Latin American countries to protect the lives of its citizens or at some distant time when the security of the United States might be threatened. On the other hand, it was apparent that the wellspring of anti-Americanism that Sandino had tapped had to be diverted. In the United States, the Monroe Doctrine was viewed as a declaration of independence from Europe, a warning to the Old World to keep hands off the New. In Latin America, it was viewed as Washington's declaration that the Western Hemisphere was the private preserve of the United States, its sphere of influence, in which it could do as it pleased. Hughes, Kellogg, Stimson, and the presidents they served all came to understand the need to divest the Monroe Doctrine of the blatantly imperialist overtones that Theodore Roosevelt had contributed in 1904 when his notorious corollary claimed for the United States the right to exercise police power to prevent "wrong-doing" in the hemisphere.

In 1928 the undersecretary of state, J. Reuben Clark, prepared a long memorandum, published in 1930, in which he denied that the right claimed in the Roosevelt Corollary derived from the Monroe Doctrine. More significantly, neither Clark nor his superiors was prepared to renounce the right to intervene—and Latin America would settle for nothing less from the United States. In the 1920s, the government of the United States perceived itself to be retreating from the imperialism of Roosevelt, Taft, and Wilson in the Caribbean, but the rest of the world was less convinced. An American military presence remained in Cuba, Haiti, and Panama, and American business interests grew throughout the region. Puerto Rico was still an American possession with no prospect of statehood. Nonetheless, sensitivity to Latin American fears and aspirations had penetrated the thinking of elites in the United States. Washington's policymakers were increasingly willing to meet with their Latin American counterparts to negotiate the terms under which the United States might be both hegemon *and* Good Neighbor.

II

Revolution in China ran roughly parallel to revolution in Mexico. The Ch'ing dynasty had collapsed in 1911, only months after Díaz had fallen. Both revolutions swept forward on promises of social reform that threatened the interests and privileges of foreigners. Like most revolutions, success against the initial target was followed by factionalism among the revolutionaries and the emergence of strongmen. In striking contrast to his policy of "watchful waiting" in Mexico, Woodrow Wilson had moved quickly to recognize the Peking government of Yuan Shih-k'ai—despite the fact that Yuan, like his Mexican counterpart, was responsible for the murder of his principal rival.

Order was not maintained long during the first decade of the Republic of China. Yuan became its first president in January 1912, but was never committed to the reformist principles of Sun Yat-sen's Kuomintang (Nationalist) party, or to a republican form of government. Within a few years of the inauguration of his government he had dissolved the parliament, used force to disperse the opposition, and attempted unsuccessfully to reestablish imperial rule, with himself as emperor. His death in 1916 removed the last semblance of national unity, civil strife intensified, and various regions of China came under the control of local warlords. When the Harding administration arrived in Washington, the Peking government controlled only parts of North China, and changes in its leadership, reflecting shifting coalitions among northern warlords, resembled a game of musical chairs.

Throughout the chaos in China there was, however, one unifying theme. Chinese intellectuals—broadly defined to include everyone with a high school education—were intensely anti-imperialist, desperately eager to rid their country of the hated "unequal treaties." Beginning with the Treaty of Nanking (1842) after their defeat in the Opium War, the Chinese had been forced to sign a series of treaties conceding special privileges to foreigners that infringed on China's sovereignty. The Chinese had lost control of their tariff, were forced to exempt foreigners from their legal system and to tolerate foreign military forces in their cities and territorial waters. Parts of China were under the de facto control of other nations, in so-called spheres of influence. The rich mineral resources of Manchuria were exploited by the Russians and the Japanese —and denied to the Chinese. Demand for the revision of the unequal treaties became the symbol of Chinese national aspirations. But China's disunity underscored its weakness, and the Great Powers ignored Chinese demands.

Signs of the ability of nationalist intellectuals to mobilize mass support had appeared in 1905 in an anti-American boycott in response to mistreatment of Chinese in the United States and the discriminatory exclusion of Chinese who wished to go there. Far more impressive and enduring were the results of the May Fourth Movement, triggered in 1919 by news that Chinese diplomats at the Paris Peace Conference had failed to regain control of the former German sphere of influence in Shantung. Hundreds of thousands of students took to the streets of Peking and other Chinese cities to protest Japanese imperialism and the impotence of their government. After the initial storm subsided, Chinese intellectuals concluded that nothing short of the transformation of Chinese civilization was necessary: The old order would have to be destroyed before China could become a modern nation-state able to command respect from the world. Widespread demands for social and intellectual change brought a new responsiveness to Western ideas, including Marxism and Leninism, and also the ideas of the great American philosopher John Dewey, who was lecturing at Peking University when the May Fourth Movement erupted.

In the realm of ideas, major transformations usually occur glacially. Change began in Peking, where intellectual leaders like Ch'en Tu-hsiu and Hu Shih pressed for educational reform and social change: educate the masses, simplify the language, elevate women, workers, peasants. No longer would men like Ch'en and Hu allow Chinese to entertain the conceit that they could attain Western wealth and power by copying Western technology while preserving Chinese traditions. "Westernization" was no longer an unacceptable price for modernization. Slowly these new approaches pressed against walls of tradition in the universities and in the cities, hardly touching the larger rural society. In the political realm, the

May Fourth Movement seemed to accomplish little other than the intimidation of the more blatantly pro-Japanese leaders. Disunity persisted, north against south, one southern warlord against another, one northern warlord against another. The great opportunity offered by the Washington Conference presented politically mobile Chinese with another round of frustration. Chinese political factions could not even unite long enough to send a delegation all could support. How could China get other nations to take its demands seriously?

Gradually, Sun Yat-sen and the Kuomintang, operating out of Canton, provided a rallying point. The American government had long since lost interest in Sun, who was generally viewed in Washington as an irresponsible visionary, an inveterate conspirator incapable of the kind of leadership China required. Assistance from the Japanese, whom Sun had once courted, was no longer feasible. If, as seemed likely, foreign assistance would be necessary for Sun's new dream of uniting China by force, to whom could he turn?

Once, years before, Sun had written to congratulate Lenin on his successful revolution in Russia. Now, as Sun and other Chinese leaders despaired, Soviet Russia came to their aid. Marxism was little understood or appreciated in China in the early 1920s, but Lenin's theories of imperialism and the anti-imperialist rhetoric of Soviet leaders proved enormously alluring. Ch'en Tu-hsiu went on from the thought of John Dewey and Bertrand Russell to Marxism-Leninism, helping to create and initially leading the Chinese Communist party. Soviet agents combed China looking for potential allies, and found Sun Yat-sen and the Kuomintang receptive.

Conceding that China was not ripe for communism, Soviet Russia agreed to help Sun toward a revolution of the "national bourgeoisie," as Sun's followers were designated by Moscow. In 1923 Soviet agents helped him to reorganize the Kuomintang from a party designed to function in a parliamentary government to a conspiratorial party along the lines of the Soviet Communist party, designed to seize and control power in a one-party state. They persuaded Sun to ally with the infant Chinese Communist party as well as with Soviet Russia. Sun's military aide, Chiang Kai-shek, was sent to Moscow to study the organization of the Red Army, and the Comintern sent a brilliant political organizer, Michael Borodin, to Canton. Chiang returned to become superintendent of the Whampoa Military Academy, where he was assisted ably in the training of officers by Chou En-lai, a young Communist intellectual responsible for political indoctrination. Borodin served as Sun's adviser and also established a school for training political cadres in the art of mobilizing the masses. In addition, in 1924 the Russians signed a convention with the Peking government surrendering some of the privileges of the unequal treaties—and further ingratiating themselves with Chinese patriots.

To all these developments the American government responded with indifference at best and occasional hostility. As Sun prepared to march north, the United States and the other Washington Conference signatories clung to the hated symbols of imperialism, the privileges exacted from nineteenth-century China by force. When Sun attempted to seize the customs surplus at Canton, to deny it to the Peking government which had only a nominal presence there, the powers, including the United States, sent warships to warn him away. In the United States there was little awareness of what was going on in China—and probably even less interest.

Hughes and his adviser on Chinese affairs, J. V. A. MacMurray, maintained toward China the same legalistic insistence on order and respect for international obligation that had handicapped dealings between the United States and Mexico's Obregón—an attitude that was, in effect, counterrevolutionary. In 1923 and 1924 there was no compelling reason for the United States to modify its policy. There was little public sense of Americans enjoying imperial privilege in China, or that these privileges might prove costly, in blood as well as treasure, to retain.

Early in 1924 the American minister to China, Jacob Gould Schurman, wrote to the new president, Calvin Coolidge, alerting him to Sun's resurgence. He was critical of Sun, whom he described as a cross between "William Jennings Bryan and a red-hot East-side socialist in New York,"[2] but warned Coolidge that Sun would have to be reckoned with. Schurman was mostly bemused by reports that Soviet influence was growing and that Sun was becoming a Bolshevik. But one young

American diplomat in Canton, J. C. Huston, the first American to undertake a serious study of the Chinese Communist movement, argued that Soviet tactics in East Asia might succeed: Soviet propaganda was stressing anti-imperialism, blaming all the ills of the region on foreign imperialists, a tune that resonated well with the resentments of Chinese intellectuals. Sun died early in 1925. Nothing happened.

The explosion came in May. On May 30, 1925, an incident arising out of a strike against Japanese-owned textile mills in Shanghai led to a spontaneous outburst of anti-imperialist sentiment that raged through China, reaching the countryside as well as the cities, affecting peasants and workers as well as students. Unlike 1919, in 1925 there were trained agitators serving the Kuomintang-Communist alliance available to fan the flames and to give focus to Chinese demands. China would settle for nothing less than treaty revision, an end to the unequal treaties, to the presence of foreign troops on Chinese soil and foreign gunboats in Chinese waters. Stubbornly, MacMurray argued against concessions in the face of threats. To yield, he insisted, would encourage irresponsible actions by Chinese infected with "various Bolshevik and juvenile nationalistic influences."[3]

To reject Chinese demands as MacMurray advised, to respond to the calls of the American business community in Shanghai for a show of force, was not an option Kellogg and Coolidge could long contemplate. Neither Congress nor public opinion would tolerate old-fashioned gunboat diplomacy, as events in Central America and Mexico were revealing. Indeed, there had been calls for the withdrawal of American gunboats and troops from China earlier in the decade, and it would require only the use of them to raise another such outcry. The American people were in no mood to use force against an underdeveloped country so that a few American businessmen and missionaries might enjoy profit and privilege abroad. Once again, the scene was set for a retreat from imperialism.

The principal remaining problem was to find a government to which the United States could yield. Chiang's forces began the Northern Expedition in July 1926. In the fall and winter they defeated warlord forces in the south and in the Yangtze Valley. By December the British indicated their willingness to revise the unequal treaties. Kellogg followed suit in January 1927. In February, a few weeks after the unanimous Senate resolution urging the peaceful settlement of Mexican-American differences, the U.S. House of Representatives overwhelmingly (226 to 43) passed the Porter Resolution. It called for negotiations to grant the Chinese the treaty revisions they demanded. There would be no war to retain the privileges of empire, no casualties, no tears. What could be retained through negotiation would be kept; what had to be fought for would be abandoned.

Preoccupation with the military campaign and internal struggles for control of the revolution delayed negotiations. In March, a Communist-led uprising facilitated Chiang's conquest of Shanghai. A few days later, Kuomintang troops occupied Nanking. Shanghai, with its large international settlement, had been taken without serious incident. In Nanking, however, Kuomintang troops attacked foreigners and foreign property, including the consulates of Great Britain, Japan, and the United States. They murdered several foreigners, among them the American vice-president of Nanking University. The looting and killing did not stop until the attackers were bombarded by American and British gunboats. Suddenly MacMurray's approach seemed less unattractive and Kellogg's policy of attempting to befriend Chinese nationalism was in jeopardy.

The events that followed were extraordinarily confusing to the men in Washington. Rumors abounded that the incidents in Nanking had been a deliberate effort by unknown forces to embarrass Chiang. A great power struggle exploded within the Kuomintang in April. Nonetheless, the three major powers, Great Britain, Japan, and the United States, held Chiang responsible and demanded that he pay reparations, punish those guilty of committing the outrages, apologize, and give assurances there would be no further incidents. American and Japanese leaders restrained the British from submitting an even harsher document. No sooner had Chiang received these demands than he ordered the arrest and massacre of Communists and labor leaders in Shanghai. Ignoring the powers, Chiang chose to consolidate his control of the revolution, eliminating the Communists and Soviet influence before Stalin could eliminate him.

By summer the White Terror had swept Kuomintang-controlled China. The surviving Communists had fled to the hills; Borodin and the rest of the Soviet advisers, accompanied by members of the Kuomintang Left, had fled the country. MacMurray was instructed to negotiate with Chiang's representatives, but factional struggles within the Kuomintang continued to disrupt the Nanking government. It was March 1928, a year after the Nanking incident, before Chiang was ready to negotiate a settlement.

Chiang accepted American terms; MacMurray grudgingly expressed regret for the naval bombardment in which American gunboats had participated; and the Nanking incident was resolved. Still, the United States withheld recognition, awaiting the outcome of the Northern Expedition. Could Chiang's forces oust the powerful Japanese-backed warlord, Chang Tso-lin, from Peking and the Northeast?

The Japanese Army preempted the battle between the two Chinese armies. In May, Japanese forces in Shantung attacked Kuomintang troops in Shantung, undermining the efforts of Japanese statesmen who saw Chiang as a moderate nationalist and bulwark against communism in Asia. When the government in Tokyo tried to retrieve the situation by ordering Chang Tso-lin to return to Manchuria and concede to the Kuomintang all of China south of the Great Wall, the Japanese Army assassinated Chang in an abortive effort to seize direct control of Manchuria. In the ensuing confusion Sino-Japanese understanding proved impossible, and the Chinese were forced to turn to the United States as the most benign of the imperialists.

Without illusions about Kuomintang unity or the real as opposed to nominal authority of Chiang's government, Kellogg chose to interpret the successful conclusion of the Northern Expedition as evidence that the Kuomintang had established itself as the de facto government of all China. Coolidge declared the Chinese Revolution to be a worthy imitation of the American Revolution, an entirely praiseworthy effort by the Chinese to unite their country and free it from foreign control—and both sides were ready to negotiate treaty revision. In July 1928 the United States and China signed a new treaty granting tariff autonomy to China and containing a mutual guarantee of most-favored-nation treatment. The signing of the treaty constituted recognition of Chiang's government and reestablished the position of the United States as China's principal foreign friend.

Americans had enjoyed imperial privileges in China since the mid-nineteenth century. They had worked in collusion with more aggressive imperial powers to obtain these privileges through the creation of the treaty system, and few were eager to surrender them. Although many missionaries believed that their cause was best served by capitulating to Chinese nationalist aspirations, few businessmen were ready to subject themselves to the vagaries of Chinese law and administration. The government of the United States was slow to recognize the imperatives of the situation, slow to respond to Chinese nationalism. When the violence in China finally impinged on the consciousness of American leaders, they understood almost immediately that the United States would have to yield. The ability of the Kuomintang and the Communists to mobilize the masses meant that retention of the privileges of empire would require the sustained use of force by the Great Powers in China, would mean American casualties—and that was not a price the American people or their leaders were willing to pay. Instead they retreated, sought rapprochement with Kuomintang China, and viewed themselves once more as "champions of the sovereign rights of China."

III

Even more remote from immediate American interests was the revolution in Russia. Initially, when the tsar's government was overthrown in March 1917, Wilson and his advisers were pleased, sympathetic to the revolutionaries. Wilson might have seen parallels with his own career and thinking in those of Paul Miliukov, the professorial intellectual who led the Kadet party in the Provisional Government. But when the Bolsheviks seized power in November, the response in Washington was very different. The appeal of Lenin and his followers to the masses, over the heads of their leaders, was threatening, as were Bolshevik tenets on property. Lenin's determination to withdraw Russia from the war, to sign a separate peace with Germany, further outraged Wilson as well as Russia's allies in Europe. Wilson perceived Lenin as more despicable than Huerta—and far more dangerous.

Among Wilson's advisers there were men like Secretary of State Robert Lansing who were eager to intervene in Russia to destroy the Bolshevik regime. Wilson was not, but he was probably second to none in his mistrust of the Bolsheviks. He never conceded the legitimacy of Lenin's government and would not extend recognition. He sent American troops on expeditions to northern Russia, where they remained until June 1919, and to Siberia, where they remained until April 1920. His reasons were complex and American forces were instructed not to interfere in the Russian civil war, but their presence and activities on Russian soil worked to the disadvantage of the Bolsheviks. Wilson understood the effect of the American military presence—and was not much troubled.

Despite the hostility of its erstwhile allies, the Bolshevik regime survived and sought to establish relations with the Great Powers. Lenin was eager for recognition, eager to come to terms with the United States. Like the Chinese, the new Russian leaders saw the remote Americans as the least dangerous of the imperialist powers. They were prepared to offer Americans economic concessions in return for development assistance and political acceptance. Wilson was offended by the idea, openly promoted by Lenin, that American goodwill could be bought. To the end of Wilson's tenure, recognition of the Bolshevik regime was withheld and contacts remained minimal. Wilson's policy toward Russia was not contested in the election of 1920. Political elites and businessmen were near unanimity in despising the Bolsheviks and opposing recognition of their government.

In July 1920 the Wilson administration finally removed wartime restrictions on trade with Russia, but imposed new obstacles, such as a prohibition against long-term credits, that left trade with the Bolsheviks more difficult than that with more favored nations. In August Wilson's secretary of state spelled out the ideological basis for nonrecognition, intending to bind successor administrations until the Soviet state changed its stripes. First, the Bolsheviks had come to power by force and were therefore not representative of the Russian people. Second, having refused to repay loans to the Provisional Government, the Bolsheviks could not be trusted to meet their international obligations. Third, Bolshevik efforts to stir revolution worldwide were evidence of their hostility to all existing governments.

Soviet leaders gave up hope of a breakthrough while Wilson remained in the White House, but were optimistic about doing business with the incoming Harding administration. Within the limits of their understanding of American political culture, they hoped the Republicans would be more responsive to economic inducement. Vaguely, as always, Harding seemed interested. A number of prominent Republicans, including Borah, vocal as always, favored recognition; but Hughes did not—and he prevailed.

Hughes would not ignore Soviet repudiation of the obligations of its predecessors. The U.S. government had extended a total of $187 million in credits to the Provisional Government. American citizens had purchased approximately $107 million in tsarist bonds. All these debts were brushed aside by Moscow. Moreover, the Soviet government confiscated American-owned property valued at nearly $350 million. And Hughes would not tolerate Soviet support for an American Communist party dedicated to the overthrow of the government of the United States. If American protests were to no avail, then the government of the United States would use the only weapons available to it: nonrecognition and discriminatory trade practices. Soviet expressions of bewilderment at the apparent hostility of the American government were ingenuous, at best.

For the United States in the 1920s, the revolution in Russia was of little relevance. As Harding and Hughes took hold in Washington, the Soviets posed no threat to the security of the United States, and they were of minimal economic importance. Despite the Red Scare in the closing months of the Wilson administration, despite the antiradicalism widespread in the country, American Communists frightened few. Their presence and the existence of the Soviet regime might serve as useful instruments for reactionary forces in American society, but there was little genuine concern—and thus little interest in Soviet Russia. There were no compelling forces for change in the policy Harding had inherited from Wilson, and that policy was not changed.

Still, the Soviet leaders reached out to American businessmen, hoping to exploit the profit motive for first political and then development purposes. In the course of the 1920s they had considerable success, especially in obtaining American financing and technology for Russian modernization. The persistent inability of the American government to harness foreign economic policy to political policy worked to Soviet advantage.

Two early concessions granted by the Soviets to Americans are interesting because of their obvious political motivation. Exploitation rights in historic Russian territory *under Japanese occupation* were offered to American capitalists. The first of these also provides a ludicrous example of the poverty of Soviet intelligence activities. One Washington Vanderlip, mistaken for his distant relative, Frank Vanderlip, a powerful New York financier, was granted exclusive coal, oil, and fisheries rights for a large chunk of Siberia. Vanderlip, in return, would presumably bring his friends in the Harding administration around to recognition, and the American government would support the Vanderlip concession and Soviet sovereignty against Japan. Vanderlip had no contacts in Washington—and nothing happened.

Harry Sinclair, an oilman with scandalously close ties to one of Harding's cronies, was given the second of these concessions. He signed a contract with the Far Eastern Republic, an allegedly autonomous entity, on the eve of its absorption into the Union of Soviet Socialist Republics. Sinclair was to develop the oil resources of north Sakhalin, an island claimed by the Soviets but occupied by the Japanese. Clearly, when Lenin spoke of contradictions among the capitalist powers leading inevitably to conflicts among them, he was prepared to hasten the process. But for all his influence, Sinclair could deliver no more than Vanderlip. All hope for the project vanished with Harding's death and the revelations of Sinclair's involvement in the Teapot Dome scandal.

After Lenin's death, several hundred more concession contracts were signed by Soviet authorities and American capitalists. All of these appear to have been inspired by the desire to obtain capital and technology rather than to engage the American government as a surrogate for Soviet interests against its foreign adversaries. The Soviet Amtorg Trading Corporation maintained an office in New York and purchased large quantities of American products. By 1930, Americans led all exporters to the Soviet state with 25 percent of the market. By 1928, a fourth of all foreign investment in Soviet Russia was also American. Averell Harriman, a central figure in Cold War relations between the United States and the Soviet Union, received a billion-dollar manganese concession. The Hammer family, Armand and his father Julius, opened a pencil factory in the Soviet Union and diversified their efforts with an asbestos mining contract and art dealing. Major corporations like DuPont, General Electric, and International Harvester signed agreements with the Soviet government for trade and the transfer of technology. Hundreds of American engineers, perhaps a thousand, agricultural and steel industry specialists, went to the Soviet Union in the 1920s to help modernize the Soviet economy.

The Ford Motor Company also developed strong links with Soviet Russia. In 1925, more than a third of the tractors exported by Ford went to the Soviets. By 1927, 85 percent of the tractors used by Russian farmers had been built by Ford. In 1929, Henry Ford signed a contract to facilitate the creation of a Soviet auto and truck industry, enabling the Russians to create a fair imitation of his Model A.

Obviously, American capital and technology contributed enormously to the development of the Soviet economy in the 1920s. It was probably essential to the success of the first Five Year Plan. Equally obvious is the fact that the government of the United States, despite widespread hostility to Bolshevism, made no effort to prevent the transfer of important technology to the Soviet state. In peacetime it was not the practice of the American government to coordinate trade with political policy—and it was just beginning to make an awkward effort to persuade bankers to subordinate their loans to what Washington perceived as the national interest. Moreover, the experience of dealing with a state-controlled economy was a new one, and few American officials anticipated the way in which such an economy could be manipulated for political ends. The ideological assumptions that underlay American abhorrence of Bolshevism, especially the commitment to "free enterprise," precluded the development of an effective foreign economic policy.

The limits of American hostility to the Bolshevik state were apparent also in the response to the famine that struck Russia at the conclusion of the civil war in 1921. Herbert Hoover, probably dreaming that American aid would win the hearts and minds of the Russian people and wean them away from Bolshevism, orchestrated a magnificent relief effort. Raising $50 million from private charities and the federal government, Hoover provided food, clothing, and medicine for an estimated 10 million Russians. Hoover's extraordinary performance strengthened the Soviet government—indeed may have saved it—and won for him its "deepest gratitude," however shortlived.

Interest in recognition of the Soviet regime remained slight through the 1920s, despite the fact that by 1925 England, France, Germany, Italy, and Japan had established formal relations with Moscow. Borah, Lamont, and most elements of the peace movement favored recognition, but it was not their primary cause. Even after the Soviets adhered to the Kellogg Pact, opposition to recognition was too strong to permit advocates to overcome the inertia in Washington. Department of State specialists in Soviet affairs were hostile to the Soviet government, as were Hoover and his aides at the Department of Commerce. They received powerful support from patriotic societies like the American Legion and the Daughters of the American Revolution. More significant was the opposition to recognition that was organized by the Catholic Church and the American Federation of Labor. The Church became intensely hostile to the Bolsheviks after the execution of its vicar general in Russia in 1923. The A.F. of L. perceived itself as serving the interests of a free labor force and had few illusions about the well-being of the proletariat in the Soviet state. Major business organizations, despite the opportunism of some of their members, also strongly opposed recognition—until the Depression led to a frantic search for markets.

Soviet attitudes toward private property, the freedom of workers, and religion were only part of the reason for the tension between Moscow and Washington. Probably more important to government officials were the activities of the Comintern, created in 1919 to coordinate revolutionary activities around the world. The Soviet government on the one hand sought and generally succeeded in establishing state to state relationships, and on the other sought to subvert governments around the world by manipulating national Communist parties for the ends of the Soviet state. Needless to say, government officials around the world viewed Comintern activities dimly.

The fact that the Comintern botched most of what it touched and had its only notable success in Outer Mongolia eased the threat, but indignation persisted. Stalin maintained effective control over the American Communist party throughout his years as the Soviet leader, and the absurd positions to which he periodically forced it to adhere precluded it from ever becoming a serious force in American politics. Nonetheless, Comintern efforts fueled opposition to recognition. It took new leadership in America, amid world economic crisis and the growing threat of Japanese militarism, to reverse American attitudes and policy toward the Soviet Union.

In the 1920s the American government remained unfriendly toward the Soviet state, but aided it in time of famine and allowed private interests virtually free rein to assist in the modernization of the Soviet economy. Stimson in 1929 offered the Soviet government gratuitous advice during a Sino-Soviet clash in Manchuria. In brief, the Bolsheviks were viewed with contempt rather than fear. All American leaders would have liked to see the Bolshevik regime disappear; none feared it enough during the 1920s to advocate any action to eliminate it. As the economic power of the United States grew, it penetrated even the Soviet state and influenced the development of that country. The larger role of the United States in world affairs in the 1920s is as evident in the Soviet Union as anywhere else in the world—and in few places was it more benign.

IV

The greatest concern of Woodrow Wilson and Allied leaders in 1919 had been the containment of German power. Wilson had understood the need to reintegrate Germany in a stable Europe if the peace won at such great cost from 1914 to 1918 was to endure. Apprehension about the threat of Bolshevism to the east may have intensified his concern, but the problem of postwar policy toward Germany was paramount whether the Soviet system survived or not. Stability in Europe, world peace, the long-term interest of the United States depended on a settlement acceptable to Germany as well as to the victors. To that end Wilson had been willing to sign a defensive alliance with Great Britain and France, as well as lead the United States into the League of Nations.

On almost all counts, Wilson failed. The peace terms imposed on Germany were harsher than he had wished and resented bitterly by most Germans. The alliance was never ratified by the U.S. Senate, nor did the United States join the League. And as the months passed, his concerns seemed excessive. When Harding and Hughes took charge of American policy, they saw a Weimar Republic in Germany that threatened no one. The German economy was a shambles, and the vaunted German military power of a few years earlier dismantled. Great Britain and France dominated Europe. The German navy and German ambitions in the Caribbean, worrisome to American leaders in the years preceding the World War, had disappeared. In 1921 it was difficult for Harding and Hughes to perceive Germany as a major concern.

France did not have the Atlantic to separate it from Germany, nor the demographic and industrial indicators that suggested long-term hegemony over continental Europe. French leaders knew that, left unchecked, Germany would recover quickly. They knew that they could not rely on the United States or Great Britain—and aid from both had been essential to stop the kaiser's forces in 1918. The answer for France was reparations. If the profits of German industry were taxed heavily and that wealth transferred from the German to the French state, France could maintain its edge. German resources, technology, and energy could be harnessed to sustain

French power. And in May 1921, the Reparations Commission established at the peace conference concluded that Germany would have to pay $33 billion, of which France would receive 52 percent. There was little expectation of collecting it all; in large part, the figure was designed to meet the expectations of the Allied public. Less than $13 billion was to be collected in the first fifteen years, during which Allied occupation of the Rhineland might be expected to function as an effective means of coercion. Nonetheless, a German state deprived of nearly a billion dollars a year would not soon threaten France. In addition, the French economy would be boosted by half that amount. In sum, the schedule of reparations on which the French insisted at the end of the war was not merely a matter of vindictiveness, but more important, a promising means of protecting the security of France.

French hopes foundered on German recalcitrance. The reparations were deemed excessive by German leaders and most of their people. The war guilt clause justifying the reparations, holding Germany and its allies uniquely responsible for the war, was also rejected by most Germans—and by many analysts in the victorious countries. The German government paid on schedule in 1921. Most economic historians today argue that Germany had the means to continue payments. In 1922, however, Germany defaulted. German leaders across the political spectrum were unwilling to continue reparations payments, certainly not on the scale demanded of them. In part, they objected to reparations as an injustice. Of greater importance was their unwillingness to face the domestic political consequences of imposing taxes to raise the necessary money. Who would be taxed to send money abroad? Could any leader who imposed so heavy a tax burden on his people hope to survive when there was always another leader calling for resistance? Every German leader, including the highly respected Gustav Stresemann, sought revision of the terms of the Treaty of Versailles to relieve Germany of the price of defeat.

France turned to the United States and Great Britain for support, and was not happy with the responses. The Americans professed to see the reparations question as an economic rather than a political question; they feared European efforts to tie reparations to war debts and ultimately to leave the bill for the war in the hands of the American taxpayer. In Washington, the Wilsonian conception of dealing with Germany through reintegration persisted. France should be generous with Germany and realize that a prosperous Germany would be a safe Germany: a fat German would be a good German. Like Wilson, Hughes—and Lamont—favored moderate revision to gain greater German acceptance. If, however, the Europeans would not behave sensibly, the outcome was viewed as less important to American interests in Harding's era than it had been in 1919. Across the channel, the British government had returned to its traditional policy of seeking to balance its most powerful European neighbors. Allied with France, it sought German goodwill so that it need fear neither as it looked to its empire and the stiff competition provided by the United States. Functionally, British attitudes also favored treaty revision to win over the Germans. France's allies among the small successor states of Eastern Europe were of little value. Belgian support counted for little. France was isolated.

In France, the military demanded occupation of the Ruhr, seizure of the heart of the German coal and steel industry. The idea was to operate Ruhr industry for the benefit of the French economy in lieu of reparations—or force the Germans to pay. Contingency plans were ready, and the Germans knew it. The forces for confrontation on both sides prevailed, and in January 1923 the test of wills began as French and Belgian forces occupied the Ruhr and the German government organized passive resistance throughout the area.

The French occupation of the Ruhr was condemned in the United States by the peace movement, journals like the *Nation* —and Senator Borah. Borah called the invasion "utterly brutal and insane" and was quoted and endorsed by the *Nation*.[3] French action ran counter to the Harding administration's conviction that German prosperity, based on the administrative and territorial integrity of Germany, was France's best hope for security. Probably no event of the 1920s contributed more to the arousal of American sympathy for the defeated enemy—or to a growing sense that French militarism was the greatest threat to the peace of Europe. Perhaps most striking was widespread criticism of the administration's alleged indifference to the Ruhr crisis. Borah warned that unless the United States responded vigorously, a new world war would begin.

Hughes had seen the crisis coming and was eager to head it off. He perceived revolution simmering in Germany. Whether the Germans swung radically left or right mattered less than the impact revolution would have on European stability, the principal aim of American policy. Hughes was restrained before and after the invasion by the unwillingness of first Harding and then Coolidge to risk confrontation with Congress. Even when it was clear there was strong support in Congress, in the press, and in the business community for some kind of action, American political leaders were reluctant to concede the relevance of reparations payments to American economic interests for fear of being maneuvered into an unpopular reduction of war debts. Moreover, neither Hughes nor Hoover was willing to offer the kind of political commitment that would have given substance to American advice.

As a result, the administration persisted in its tactic of pushing American bankers forward, working from behind their skirts to impose an American solution on the problem. In December 1922 Hughes proposed the creation of an independent committee of financial experts, presumably Anglo-American, which would devise a fair plan for reparations payments. He was too late then, but the idea was revived successfully by the British less than a year later—after nine months of French occupation, passive resistance, and hyperinflation had all but destroyed the German government.

German resistance succeeded in raising the cost of the occupation, but Raymond Poincaré, the French leader, perceived no choice but to press on. However questionable the French economy was soon revealed to be, in 1923 it was infinitely stronger than that of the Weimar Republic. Financing the resistance further undermined the shaky German currency and in a few months it collapsed, resulting in devastating hyperinflation. No one in Germany seemed to have the will or the knowledge to save the mark. The foundations of the fragile Republic were shaken, and both its survival and even the unity of Germany seemed at stake by the summer of 1923. In September, under the leadership of Stresemann, the German government surrendered. Resistance had failed to drive the French out. Neither the Americans nor the British had come to the rescue. It was time for a tactical retreat in the struggle for treaty revision. It was essential to reconstruct German finances—not to facilitate reparations payments, but to serve the German state.

The French, however, were unable to benefit from the "success" of their occupation of the Ruhr. There was no way to press their advantage to extract significant revenue out of Germany, in cash or in kind. They too were ready for tactical retreat such as provided by the proposed committee of experts. Poincaré attempted to limit the terms of inquiry to Germany's immediate capacity to pay, hoping to preserve the right to resume full payments in the future, but Hughes balked. The United States, having emerged as the dominant financial power in the world, held the key hand. The French, Germans, and British all wanted American participation, needed American participation, and were forced to play by American rules. In January 1924 the experts assembled in Paris to begin their inquiry. The chairman of the committee was Charles G. Dawes, an American banker.

Despite the pretense that the American representatives on what came to be known as the Dawes Committee were acting as private citizens, the government of the United States left nothing to chance. Hughes and his advisers selected the American participants, Dawes and Owen D. Young (chairman of the General Electric Corporation). Dawes and Young were carefully briefed by Hughes and Hoover. They were provided with background materials collected by the Departments of State and Commerce—and with advisers from those departments. They went to Paris to serve the interests of their government, which retained the freedom to deny responsibility for their actions.

As the Dawes Committee assembled, a financial crisis began in France that ultimately left the French government unable to resist the course which the Americans and British set. France, like Germany, had failed to resolve domestic differences on the question of distribution of the tax burden for postwar reconstruction. French leaders had hoped to avoid a divisive battle by squeezing the costs from Germany and sparing their constituencies additional taxes. By January 1924 it was clear that Germany would not provide the needed funds, that taxation had been postponed too long; the franc collapsed. The French government desperately needed an international loan. Its financial adviser was none other than J. P. Morgan and Company, specifically Dwight Morrow who, with Lamont, would decide whether, when, and how much Morgan might lend. The Morgan partners were highly sympathetic to France's plight, but banking is never intentionally a nonprofit operation. Potential investors had to be assured of a favorable business climate. Specifically, Lamont insisted he be assured that France would not resort to force to collect reparations before Morgan would lend to France. Only a peaceful Germany and a stable Europe would provide the climate desired.

When the French finally capitulated to Morgan's terms, Lamont cleared the loan with Hughes and the pieces of the pattern Lamont and Hughes sought to create began to fall into place. A few weeks later, in April 1924, the Dawes Committee reported its plan which, when implemented at a conference in London that summer, resulted in a de facto scaling down of the German reparations burden, a payment schedule which required Germany to begin small-scale payments immediately and increase payments as its economy improved. Money for the payments would come in part from loans floated by J. P. Morgan and Company, from which the British, Belgians, and French could also anticipate loans so long as the right to impose sanctions on Germany was renounced. Clearly, France sacrificed the most—in terms of reparations payments it might expect from Germany and the leverage French leaders desired in the event Germany reneged on the new payment schedule. France had little choice, given the attitude of the governments in Washington and London—and of the men on Wall Street and Lombard.

The American government and American bankers asked still more of their friends and potential borrowers in Europe. They were interested in seeing the development of a European

community in which the animosities of the world war, exacerbated by the Treaty of Versailles, might finally be put to rest.
They wanted assurance not only that France would withdraw
from the Ruhr and refrain from another invasion, but that
Great Britain, France, and Germany would work together to
rebuild and stabilize Europe. In January 1925, Stresemann
resubmitted his proposal for a four-power guarantee of the
German-French border. With British elaborations, Stresemann's idea became the foundation for the Locarno treaties
signed in October 1925. Belgium, France, and Germany promised to respect forever the boundaries drawn at Versailles and
to keep the Rhineland demilitarized. Additionally, they promised never to attack each other. Great Britain and Italy signed
as guarantors. Here was the negotiated settlement of the war
issues the United States sought. Now, with the approval of
their government, American bankers were ready to under-
write European recovery. Again, the French had reservations
about the value of these Anglo-American plans for their security, but Washington and Morgan and Company had left
French leaders no doubt that the Locarno arrangements, like
the Dawes Plan, were the essential requisites to the financial
aid France required. Moreover, French anxieties were as-
suaged by the integration of both Great Britain and Germany
in France's security system.

Clearly, the United States, working outside the League of
Nations, uncommitted by the Treaty of Versailles or any security arrangements with the European powers, nonetheless
played the central role in stabilizing Europe in the mid-1920s.
Conscious of American financial hegemony, the Harding and
Coolidge administrations, utilizing American bankers with
striking effectiveness—in contrast with failed efforts in China
—were able to call the tune. American loans enabled German
leaders to rebuild their nation's economy in the hope of integrating Germany into a community with its recent enemies.
American loans required France to rely on German commitment to the idea of community rather than the threat of force
for its security. As a result, the outlook for peace in Europe
was good. Tension between the United States and France over
war debts, the French invasion of the Ruhr, and France's

obstructive policies in East Asia began to decline. Relations with Great Britain and Germany prospered as well. In Europe, the American approach to world affairs was manifestly successful.

Fueled by American loans, Europe experienced a spurt of economic growth and prosperity after Locarno. Germany paid reparations, the Allies paid installments on their war debts, and all was well in the world. Americans began dreaming of a chicken in every pot, a car in every garage. The key to the success of the American vision for the world was continued world prosperity—a larger pie and a bigger piece for everyone. But the world economic system remained seriously flawed. In the post-Locarno euphoria, too much American money flowed to Germany and too much of it was used for nonproductive purposes, for paying off reparations and earlier loans. The Germans were still not taking the burden of their reparations payments on themselves, and the United States was still not importing anywhere near what the Germans had to sell to repay what they borrowed. The system depended on the continued flow of dollars across the Atlantic. Should American loans to Germany stop, the system was likely to collapse.

A second problem was the persistent German desire for treaty revision, to be relieved of reparations payments and the presence of occupying forces on German territory. Germany joined the League (1926), signed the Kellogg-Briand Pact (1928) promising not to resort to war as an instrument of national policy—and pressed for revision. In 1929, another committee of experts, again led by an American, Owen Young, lowered Germany's reparations bill and called for the evacuation of all foreign troops from the Rhineland. The Young Plan was approved early in 1929 and the last foreign troops were out of Germany by June 1930. German good behavior had won renewed respect and goodwill in Washington and European capitals. The Weimar Republic was not the Germany of the kaiser, and the world at the end of the 1920s might look to enduring peace and prosperity. Americans had every right to feel proud of the contribution of their government—and their bankers.

V

Expanding from traditional areas of economic involvement and government activity in the Caribbean and East Asia, the United States played a role of tremendous importance in Europe as well in the 1920s. American leaders had to respond to three great revolutions, begun earlier but still reverberating in the era of Harding and Coolidge. They were drawn into the principal European drama being played out in Germany. The importance of America's new stature as financial capital of the world was evident in the prominence of Lamont and his Morgan partners in Mexico, China, France, and Germany.

Perhaps most striking was the technique evolved for using nongovernmental leaders like Lamont or Morrow or Young to serve the ends of American foreign policy. Advisers to Presidents Wilson, Harding, and Hoover, some of them no strangers to Wall Street, quickly perceived the value of banker-diplomatists. In theory these men functioned as private citizens. The United States government could deny responsibility for their actions, would not be bound by their agreements. Generally the government could direct the efforts of these representatives from the private sector—select them, inform them, instruct them—almost as easily as if they had been on the payroll. And the government was able to engage in activities that, had they been official, would have aroused the wrath of special interests or congressmen at home and foreign governments abroad. The waters out there were mined and, shrewdly, while the government and people of the United States gained an education in the use and responsibilities of power, Washington sent the bankers ahead to clear the way.

The virtues of the system of reliance on the private sector for conducting public policy were balanced, however, by a flaw most evident in East Asia. However public-spirited the Morgan partners may have been, their interests and those of the American government and people did not always coincide. In such circumstances, patriotism gave way to self-interest. In East Asia, the Department of State was eager to see Lamont and the international bankers with whom he was associated lend money to the Chinese government. The government of the United States certainly did not want Morgan financing Japanese imperialism in China, facilitating Japanese exclusion of American business interests. But Lamont had no interest in lending money to a succession of shaky Chinese regimes and was delighted to lend to Japan, surely a safer investment. Indeed, Lamont used his considerable genius to circumvent all efforts by his friends in Washington to prevent Morgan loans to the Japanese government. In brief, private citizens, however gifted, are imperfect instruments of national policy, to be used sparingly and with great caution and skepticism.

Still, the central point is that the United States engaged in enormously expanded activities around the world, often spearheaded by American capital and, in Soviet Russia especially, American industry. The growth of American activity in the world was acceptable to virtually all Americans—there were no cries for a "little America" policy—so long as the use of force was not required. Congressional warnings on policy toward Mexico and China, public distaste for the war in Nicaragua, and ultimately the Kellogg-Briand Pact left no doubt in the minds of American leaders of the restraints imposed by the organized peace movement. "Tomorrow the world"—if it could be ours peacefully.

CHAPTER 5

AFTER THE FALL

I

In March 1929 Herbert Clark Hoover was inaugurated as the thirty-first president of the United States. For the previous eight years he had served Harding and Coolidge as secretary of commerce and had been a major force in shaping the domestic and foreign policies of the United States. One of the principal architects of the cooperative association of government and the private sector which had worked so well throughout the 1920s, he promised to lead the American people to new heights of prosperity. A Quaker, reluctant to use force as an instrument of power, he was the ideal choice to maintain and even expand the American empire—without tears. A prosperous America would guide the world.

The stock market responded favorably to Hoover's election and the number of Americans prepared to risk their savings —and other people's money—on the continued growth of the economy increased. Problems of shrinking agricultural markets, overextended holding companies, unproductive foreign loans were little noticed. In September, however, the market wavered. On October 23, 1929, the ticker tape at the New York Stock Exchange ran 104 minutes late as the day ended and the market fell sharply. On October 24, the market collapsed in the face of panic selling. The Great Depression had begun its withering course. As the economy stumbled, the American presence around the world began to contract.

Increasingly over the next several years, the Great Depression dominated every aspect of American life. Nothing that occurred anywhere in the world could compete for the attention of American leaders and their people. No foreign threat could compare with the danger the Depression posed to the survival of American institutions and values—to democracy in America. By 1931 even Henry Stimson, the secretary of state, was preoccupied with the search for the road to recovery.

The apparatus of foreign affairs was affected negatively by the economic crisis, but not as seriously as might have been anticipated. The number of foreign service officers fell off sharply in the early 1930s, declining by about 10 percent as those who retired or resigned went unreplaced. Pay cuts do not seem to have affected the quality of the service. Those with independent incomes, a class still overrepresented among career diplomats, hardly noticed. Others, less fortunate, were not eager to compete with the 15 million able-bodied Americans already unemployed. The resignation rate throughout the 1930s was remarkably low, barely more than 1 percent. Nonetheless, a reduced number of officers had to staff a substantial increase in American embassies and legations, up from 47 in 1920 to 58 in 1930.

Under extraordinarily adverse conditions, Department of Commerce attachés worked frenetically and futilely to promote American exports as nation after nation acted to protect home markets, as economic nationalism prevailed in the depression-wracked world markets. When American agricultural exports shrank in the late 1920s, even before the crash, the Department of Agriculture followed Commerce's lead. Beginning in 1930, Agriculture posted specialists in the embassies and legations in the hope of finding markets for a burgeoning surplus.

American military power fell off only slightly in absolute terms, but fared less well relative to increases in Japanese naval power—and was inadequate for the crisis that developed in Manchuria in 1931. U.S. Army personnel stood at 136,547 in 1933, down only about 1 percent from the average of the previous ten years. The Air Corps expanded between 1927 and 1930. Expansion stopped in 1932, but the number of planes, officers, and enlisted men was only slightly short of what had been projected in the mid-1920s. Naval leaders were pleased with the efficiency of their own air arm. On the other hand, naval and marine personnel had dropped about 4 percent in 1933 from the average for the previous decade. Worst of all, from the perspective of the admirals and the Navy League, not a single new ship was authorized during the Hoover administration. Moreover, at the London Naval Conference of 1930, the United States accepted a cruiser ratio that outraged American naval officers.

In sum, even during the Depression, the apparatus with which the United States, as a great power, maintained its interests around the world, remained in place. The collapse of the economy affected the will more than the means to act abroad as the nation turned inward to concentrate on the suffering of its own people.

II

The most obvious impact of the Great Depression on America's foreign relations came in economic affairs. As late as 1930, a number of corporations were still investing heavily overseas. Mining companies continued to expand their operations in Latin America until the bottom dropped out of commodity prices. In 1930 ITT gained control of the Peruvian telephone system, won major concessions in Chile and Rumania, and an important share of the opportunities available in Turkey and China. Trade with Soviet Russia did not decline until 1932. But in every other respect, retrenchment was sharp and painful by 1931.

As the economic situation in the United States worsened, most corporations concentrated on domestic activity. The level of world trade declined as nation after nation erected trade barriers to protect home industries. On one of the rare occasions when a thousand American economists agreed on any subject, that number petitioned Hoover with a warning against signing the Smoot-Hawley tariff of 1930. He defied their collective judgment and the retaliatory action they predicted was taken throughout the industrial world, most painfully for American exporters by Canada and Europe generally.

From 1919 to 1930 American business had invested $11.6 billion overseas. Beginning in 1931 there were no new investments, and a reverse flow began. Money previously invested in Africa, Asia, Canada, Europe, Latin America, and the Middle East was called back. In part the reverse flow was caused by the need for capital at home; in part it was withdrawn because of growing unrest overseas: Japanese actions in China; revolutions in Latin America; the economic, social, and political disintegration of Germany. American firms abroad found the climate less attractive than it had been during the 1920s and feared they could not prosper. In 1932 stock market analysts warned investors against firms with large overseas operations, but a few firms, especially in Great Britain, expanded in the face of high tariffs rather than abandon the local market.

The bankers stopped lending money to foreign governments in 1929. Congress closed the door to foreign imports in 1930. By 1931 American tourists had all but disappeared from the world's grand hotels, spas, casinos, and exotic sites. Corporate investment abroad ended. The result was an extraordinary drop in the number of dollars available abroad—a 68 percent decline in the dollars whose circulation had kept the world economic system afloat in the 1920s. Much of what was left was consumed by fixed obligations such as war debts. Virtually nothing was available for the purchase of American goods. And the whole system collapsed.

Fear that a new round of defaults would further undermine the disintegrating financial system of Europe and accelerate the rate of bank failure in the United States forced Hoover to ease his position on war debts and reparations. Neither Lamont nor Stimson had succeeded in winning him over to the cancellation side of the debate, and he had long been wary of the domestic political consequences of forgiving

U.S. Exports of Leading Manufactured Goods ($ millions)

YEAR	IRON/STEEL	MACHINERY	AUTOS/PARTS	TOTAL
1922	$136.2	$233.9	$103.2	$ 473.3
1929	200.1	604.4	541.4	1,345.9
1932	28.9	131.3	76.3	236.5

SOURCE: U.S. Department of Commerce, *The United States in the World Economy* (Washington, DC: U.S. Government Printing Office, 1943), p. 59.

America's debtors. By 1931, however, it was apparent that Germany was again on the verge of defaulting in reparations payments to France, that the French were prepared to accept financial chaos in Germany, and that the result would be a string of failures among American banks, to which the Germans were deeply indebted.

Hoover needed little instruction to recognize the danger and called for a moratorium on payment of all international debts—a none too subtle admission of the long-denied connection between war debts and reparations. The United States would claim no payments on war debts for a year if France and others would agree to forego reparations payments for a like period. It was a brave move by Hoover, doubtless long overdue. French procrastination rendered the gesture all but futile—as it likely would have been in any event. At home Hoover's action won wide approval, but the moratorium did not prevent the cycle Hoover dreaded. The horrors of the Depression intensified.

III

Hoover and many of his contemporaries had envisioned a world in which prosperity, fueled by the American economy, would mute the issues that divided nations and the peoples within them. Everyone's standard of living would rise, peace would prevail, and funds wasted on military expenditures could be put to productive use. From the moment of his election, Hoover attempted to realize that vision. In his faith in the curative powers of the American economy, his reluctance to intervene in the affairs of other nations, and his commitment to disarmament, he epitomized—perhaps was a caricature of—the American political culture of the 1920s. Certainly there were few presidential candidates whose election would have been more gratifying to the American peace movement.

Hoover was particularly displeased by the enormous sums the United States continued to spend on warships, despite the naval limitation agreement of 1922. Throughout his presidency, he was at war with the Navy League, an organization committed to the enlargement of the U.S. Navy, ostensibly to maintain American seapower in a hostile world. The Navy League had been worried by Coolidge as well, by his opposition to naval construction on economic grounds, but had gained support for its objectives after the failure of the Geneva Conference of 1927. At Geneva, poor preparation and Anglo-American differences over cruiser ratios and sizes had precluded agreement. An Anglo-French naval agreement in 1928 further irritated Americans and aided Navy League lobbyists in Congress. In February 1929 the Senate approved a bill to build fifteen new cruisers. Navy League supporters and lobbyists were ecstatic. In March 1929 Hoover became president, determined to see that not one of those fifteen cruisers was ever built.

The cruiser bill of 1929 demonstrated to the British that agreement with the United States could no longer be avoided. Great Britain too had a leader, Ramsay MacDonald, who was determined to avoid a costly arms race which Britain could not win. The United States would have to be granted parity. For three months, beginning in late January 1930, the great naval powers met in London in an effort to extend limits on shipbuilding to cruisers, destroyers, and submarines.

For the Americans and the British negotiators, the top priority was an end to Anglo-American discord. However grumpily, the British admirals were forced to approve the American demand for a rough parity in cruisers. The Japanese, French, and Italians, on the other hand, were determined to enlarge their fleets relative to the two leading naval powers. Anglo-American efforts to extend the 5:5:3 tonnage ratio applied to capital ships in the 1922 agreement to cruisers in 1930 defied reality. In 1922 the American and British battleships outweighed their Japanese rivals by approximately the 5:3 ratio the Japanese accepted. In 1930, Japanese cruiser tonnage was in fact double that of the American cruisers. The Japanese were being asked to stop building until the Americans caught up and surpassed them. Faced with Anglo-American collusion, a well-intentioned Japanese government agreed to a compromise, accepting cruiser inferiority on a 10:10:7 basis instead of the requested 10:10:6.

As is usually the case when political leaders make decisions in military affairs, the professional naval people in Great

Britain, Japan, and the United States insisted they had been betrayed. Charged with the defense of their country's interests, military leaders are rarely satisfied unless assured of a preponderance of power so great there can be no doubt of their success. A reflexive quest for assured success rather than sinister motives usually explains constant military demands for more. In 1930, as in 1922, the naval building limitation agreement provided adequately for the security of all the leading naval powers. It was of less enduring value in part because of the overweening aspirations of Japanese military leaders, and in large part because Hoover misread its significance. Unwilling to spend on "unproductive" warships, he deceived himself into believing that the London agreement ended the naval race, dispelled the fears and suspicions that bred war— and that there was no need for the United States to build even those ships allowed it under the agreement. Not even the crisis that exploded in Mukden in 1931 moved Hoover to authorize a single new ship.

IV

Relations between the United States and Japan had improved markedly as a result of the agreements reached at Washington in 1922 and the preceding agreement on the creation and modus operandi of the new China consortium. The generous American response to the earthquake disaster of 1923 may even have cushioned slightly the shock both the Japanese and Charles Evans Hughes received in 1924 when Congress overrode Hughes's efforts and passed new exclusion laws aimed at Japanese emigrants. (At Lamont's urging, J. P. Morgan and Company contributed mightily to Japan's development in the 1920s.) To be sure, the cooperative policy to which the Great Powers were committed in China broke down in the face of the Chinese revolution, and the actions of the Japanese army in Shantung in 1927 raised apprehensions. By the summer of 1931, however, American leaders were pleased and complacent about relations between Japan and the United States. Shidehara Kijuro was the Japanese foreign minister, and he was admired and respected by Western diplomats who had worked with him since the days of the Washington Conference. His policies were restrained, threatened no American interests, and suggested that he had the Japanese military under control. The success of the London Conference of 1930 persuaded Hoover and his advisers that rivalry with Japan was not going to be a concern for the foreseeable future. As the woes of the Depression multiplied at home, little thought was given to conditions in East Asia—not even to warnings that the Japanese military in Manchuria were growing restive.

The Japanese had established their presence in Manchuria in the course of defeating Russia in 1905. China retained nominal control over the region, its three northeastern provinces. For the next quarter of a century, resisting all external pressures, Japan developed Manchuria and integrated it into the Japanese economic and strategic systems. Manchuria was the front line of defense against Russia, and it was the principal and most reliable source of the iron and coal that propelled Japanese industry into its primary position in Asia. Military or civilian, moderate or extremist, all Japanese leaders, including Shidehara, viewed Manchuria as a vital interest and were committed to keeping it under Japanese control. As befitted a diplomatist, Shidehara insisted on negotiation to preserve Japan's interests. Not surprisingly, the Japanese army was frequently impatient with talk and had begun straining at the leash as Chiang Kai-shek's government began to impinge on territory Japanese officers saw as akin to a feudal fiefdom. A plot to take over Manchuria had very nearly been executed in 1928, at the time of the murder of Chang Tso-lin. The plans were still on the books in September 1931.

In March 1931 the American minister to China, Nelson T. Johnson, wrote that Manchuria was becoming more Chinese with each passing day. The Japanese army shared his assessment, and despaired of Shidehara's efforts. On the evening of September 18, 1931, Japanese troops sprang into action. To allege Chinese provocation, the Japanese set off an explosion in the vicinity of the Japanese-owned and operated South Manchuria Railroad. Responding to the "provocation," Japanese soldiers drove Chinese authorities out of the city of Mukden and began the conquest of Manchuria.

The Mukden Incident occurred at an inauspicious moment

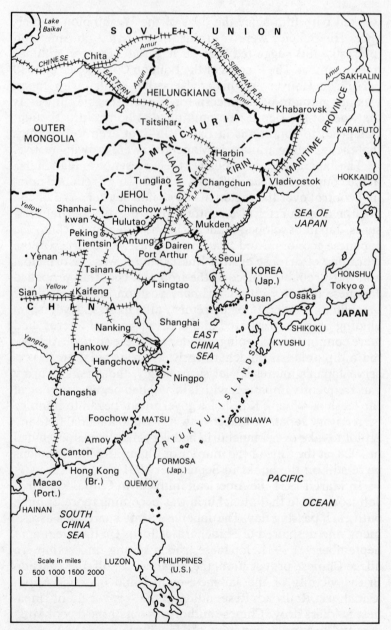

Manchuria and Adjacent Area

for the Chinese government. It was already mired in a series of domestic struggles as Kuomintang secessionists at Canton and Communist rebels in Kiangsi taxed Chiang's political and military acumen. Informed of Japanese operations at Mukden, Chiang chose to concentrate his efforts against the Communists. A campaign against the Japanese would have to wait until he had eliminated the internal threat. Attempting to localize the incident to Mukden, he ordered Chinese forces in Manchuria not to resist. On the diplomatic front, he appealed to Great Britain, the League of Nations, and the United States to stop Japan.

Deep in the throes of the Depression, the nations of the West were not quick to rally to China's support. When news of Japanese actions penetrated the gloom in Washington, American leaders prayed the incident would prove to be an isolated matter. They wanted no distraction in their search for an escape from economic stagnation, and put their faith in Shidehara.

Stimson, having little choice, was determined to give Shidehara the opportunity to halt the adverturism of the military. Consistent with the kind of advice he received from Lamont, Stimson sent gently worded notes to both the Chinese and Japanese governments asking them to end the hostilities. He carefully avoided any kind of threat that might stimulate Japanese chauvinism, play into the hands of military extremists, and undermine Shidehara and other "moderates." Shidehara sent the assurances for which Stimson hoped: Japanese troops would be recalled to the railroad zone as soon as possible. Stimson waited watchfully, hopefully.

But Shidehara had lost control, and the Japanese army continued its advance through Manchuria. With the bombing of Chinchow in early October it was clear that the army was ignoring the government in Tokyo and intended to drive Chinese forces out of Manchuria. What could the United States do? Chiang demanded that the Americans invoke the Kellogg-Briand Pact. Stimson, however, had tried that in 1929 during a Chinese-Soviet crisis and, to his embarrassment, had found the moral force of the pact of minimal value. He was not eager to jump out in front again. He and Hoover preferred to see the League of Nations take the lead and to that end were willing to allow the American consul general in Geneva to sit with the League Council. In mid-October the United States joined the League in reminding both Chinese and Japanese of their pledges when they signed the Kellogg-Briand Pact, but to no effect.

In China there was despair. Efforts to invoke the League Covenant, the Kellogg Pact, and America's sense of its role as China's champion had failed to generate sufficient external pressure on Japan. Chiang's preference for eliminating his domestic enemies before confronting Japan angered Chinese patriots. He was forced to resign as president, although he retained control of both the military and the party apparatus.

In Washington, Hoover's cabinet was forced to focus on the issue, to put the economic crisis aside for the moment and determine how the United States would respond if the Japanese army continued to defy Shidehara and seized all of Manchuria. Stimson, Hoover, and their principal advisers understood the importance of Manchuria to Japan and could empathize with Japanese irritation over Chinese challenges. Hoover's years in China, ended by the Boxer Rebellion, left him with little sympathy for that nation's plight. On the other hand, he admired Japan's process of modernization, the evidence of a progressive, efficient people. Nonetheless, Hoover considered the actions of the Japanese army to be outrageous and immoral. The Japanese had violated their pledges under the Nine-Power Treaty of 1922 and the Kellogg Pact of 1928. On the other hand, no one in the cabinet argued that important American interests were threatened in Manchuria. Moreover, the secretary of war declared that the military was not strong enough to confront Japan.

In a similar context in 1910, Theodore Roosevelt had urged President William Howard Taft not to antagonize the Japanese. Roosevelt warned that Japanese interests in Manchuria were vital and that American interests there were not. Lacking adequate military power or the public support necessary to use force in so remote a region of the world, it would be best to drop the issue. Taft's secretary of state, Philander Knox, had been repelled by Roosevelt's argument. The territory in question was Chinese and the United States would not acquiesce in Japanese imperialism. He would seek an alternative between war and surrender. In fact, Knox never found a feasible alternative. In 1931, Japanese aggression was more blatant and appeasement seemed even less attractive to Stimson than it had to Knox. But what could be done?

The strongest pressure on the Hoover administration to act against Japan came from the American peace movement. Although the movement remained divided over the relative importance of disarmament, outlawing of war, and membership in the League as the means toward a shared goal, all activists perceived the threat Japan posed to the system so laboriously constructed after the world war. If Japan could violate its commitments to the peace system with impunity, the system would collapse. Leaders of the peace movement, especially Dorothy Detzer of the Women's International League for Peace and Freedom, demanded that the United States act to stop Japan.

Stimson shared the vision of some of the leaders of the peace movement, and he perceived America's postwar role as the world's greatest power. Much like Woodrow Wilson, he had a profound sense of the need of the United States to maintain a new world order in which there would be no place for aggression. Japan had to be stopped, the peace system, the new world order, had to be preserved—but how? Hoover was adamant against the use of force. Neither Detzer nor most of the other peace organization leaders contemplated force. Stimson himself never advocated using force. And the military left no doubt that the means were not available had anyone wanted to use force to stop Japan. In October 1931, Hoover and Stimson were agreed that the United States could cooperate with the League in a campaign of moral suasion, while avoiding any League effort to defer leadership to Washington. Detzer remained suspicious that the United States had sold out to Japan, but most leaders of the peace movement were heartened by the cooperation between Washington and Geneva.

As Western leaders groped for some way short of force to stop the Japanese army, Stimson considered economic sanctions, uncertain whether they were warranted or would be effective, or of the risks such action might entail. Hoover argued that economic sanctions led inevitably to war and was unwilling to use them. Then, amid despair over American impotence, the Japanese government called for a commission of inquiry and the League Council agreed to send what came to be known as the Lytton Commission. Stimson praised the League, pledged the support of the United States, and resumed his hope that Shidehara would prevail.

On December 11, 1931, the cabinet in which Shidehara was foreign minister resigned, ending forever the era of Shidehara diplomacy. The new Japanese government quickly approved army plans to seize all of Manchuria—and the nearby province of Jehol in Inner Mongolia. By the end of the first week of January, 1932, Japanese troops controlled all of Manchuria, had entered the strategic city of Shanhaikuan at the Great Wall, and were poised to move into North China. The time for wishful thinking had passed.

One idea that had emerged in discussions between Stimson and Hoover was for the United States to issue a statement refusing to recognize the fruits of Japanese aggression. In various forms the idea had occurred to several people, in and out of the administration, but it did not seem a very promising approach and it lay in abeyance until January 7, 1932. In desperation, Stimson returned to "nonrecognition." He sent identical notes to the governments of China and Japan declaring the refusal of the United States to admit the legality of the situation in Manchuria and its unwillingness to accept any arrangements there affecting its treaty rights or those of its citizens, including those relating to the sovereignty, independence, and territorial and administrative integrity of China; nor would the United States recognize any situation brought about in violation of the Kellogg Pact. The Stimson (or Hoover-Stimson) Doctrine, as the notes were ultimately labeled, provided American leaders with a palliative for the discomfort caused by their inability and unwillingness to take more aggressive and conceivably more effective action against Japan.

Three weeks later, the Japanese navy attacked Shanghai. Japanese Marines landed in the city and advanced against Chinese military positions. Ships in the harbor unloaded salvo after salvo, rarely discriminating between soldier and civilian. Wave after wave of Japanese planes pounded residential districts. And, unlike their comrades in Manchuria, Chinese troops ignored their government's orders to retreat; they resisted stubbornly and prolonged the hostilities

The bloodshed in Shanghai, the attacks on civilians, and the proximity of a large foreign population and foreign property aroused public attention in the West to a degree that the attack on Mukden had not. In Europe especially and among foreigners in China, there had been considerable sympathy for the Japanese position in Manchuria. Chiang's regime, with its stridently nationalistic demands, had won few friends in the international settlement. Outside of missionary circles, most foreigners in China, and most diplomats who dealt with China, were prepared to accept Japanese claims of provocation and of special interests. Far fewer could condone the attack on Shanghai.

American awareness of events in Shanghai appears to have been much greater than the minimal attention the crisis in Manchuria had wrenched from a Depression-wracked public. Shanghai contained more American residents than any other Chinese city. Suddenly there was a direct danger to American lives and property. Japan had to be stopped. Even Lamont, who blamed China for the Manchurian crisis, who had found ways to assist the Japanese financially, and who opposed Stimson's efforts to increase pressure on Japan, changed course and came to Stimson's aid.

Within the American peace movement, a demand for economic sanctions boiled. A. Lawrence Lowell, president of Harvard, attempted to organize a nationwide boycott of Japanese goods, and sympathetic women refused to wear stockings made of Japanese silk (when cotton stockings proved unattractive, the nylon stocking was born). Leaders of the peace movement were as uncertain as Hoover and Stimson about the effectiveness of such actions, but were driven by a greater sense of urgency than the president. Their fears for the survival of the peace system intensified. Moreover, they perceived that failure to develop an effective nonviolent means of stopping Japan would be viewed as impotence and result in a loss of influence to organizations like the Navy League, to advocates of military preparedness, of superior American military force as the only means of stopping Japan. Economic sanctions might be the answer.

Hoover remained adamantly opposed. Lamont sent protests to his Japanese friends through his private channels, and Stimson protested officially. The secretary of state was fast losing faith in the efficacy of world public opinion. He argued for increasing the American fleet in Shanghai's harbor. He asked the president to send marines to Shanghai, both to protect Americans there and to signal Japan that the United States was not prepared to surrender its pretensions to power in East Asia. The American admirals were uneasy, fearful of a Japanese attack for which the U.S. Navy in the western Pacific was not adequately prepared. Indirectly, Nelson T. Johnson, the American minister to China, provided strong support for Stimson's position. Johnson warned that the absence of American support for Chinese resistance to Japanese aggression might result in an indiscriminate, Boxer-like rage against foreigners. Hoover accepted Stimson's recommendation, and naval and marine units moved to Shanghai.

The Japanese military was not intimidated by American gestures or moved by American protests. Lamont's friends among Japanese leaders were isolated and then assassinated as the military and civilian extremists ripped the reins of power from their hands. Japan in 1932 was in the hands of men very different from those with whom the West had cooperated in the 1920s. In the United States the peace movement slowly became demoralized by its inability to find an adequate response to Japanese militarism and its apprehension that anti-Japanese sentiment might lead to war. Stimson struggled on, groping for a way to live with his conscience, for a way to avoid appeasing Japan, for a way to save the new world order and the peace system upon which it was founded.

In February 1932 Stimson tried a new tack, a protest against Japan's actions as a violation of the Nine-Power Treaty of 1922. Despairing of European support for his maneuver, recognizing the inadvisability of a unilateral protest, he wrote an open letter to Senator William Borah, chairman of the Senate Foreign Relations Committee. In it, he called attention to the obligations Japan, like Great Britain and the United States, had accepted when signing the several treaties resulting from the Washington Conference of 1921–1922 and to the long-standing agreement among the countries concerned to preserve the territorial integrity of China. He expressed the hope that all nations would withhold recognition of arrangements resulting from violations of these agreements—and of the Kellogg Pact. Pointedly, Stimson noted that violations of treaty provisions respecting Chinese territory freed the United States from restrictions on the size of its fleet and from its pledge not to fortify its possessions in the Pacific.

The support for which Stimson hoped from Great Britain and other League Council members was never obtained. European capitals were also filled with men unwilling to bell the cat. Apart from those who sympathized with Japanese anger at evidences of Chinese nationalism, most European leaders were mindful of the superior power Japan could bring to bear in East Asia. Moreover, the Japanese had left no doubt of their willingness to use that power in pursuit of interests virtually all Japanese, including the "moderates" to whom Lamont looked, deemed vital. No European leader saw the interests of his people in China worth the price that might have to be paid to challenge Japan. In general a realism similar to that proferred by Roosevelt in 1910 prevailed in Europe. Nonetheless, in March the League Council did endorse the nonrecognition policy Stimson and Hoover advocated—too late to stop Japan from creating the puppet state of Manchukuo. The Lytton Commission began its investigation of the Mukden Incident in May 1932, but its work was futile.

The Japanese did finally terminate hostilities in Shanghai in May 1932, less under duress from the West than because Japanese military leaders never intended more than to bloody the Chinese for daring to harass Japanese interests in the city. Unexpected Chinese resistance engaged the honor of the Japanese military and prolonged what might otherwise have been a brief punitive expedition, reminding the Diet in Tokyo, when it was time for appropriations, that the navy also protected the glory of the empire. Had the Japanese had more aggressive intentions toward Shanghai, their responses to complaints about their activities in Manchuria suggest that they would not have allowed Stimson's threats or the tepid League action to deter them.

Stimson's efforts were further undermined by Hoover. The president, by May 1932, was acting with one eye toward the November election. He was in serious trouble with the American people because of the Depression, the failure of his programs for recovery, and his apparent insensitivity to the widespread suffering in the world's wealthiest country. Foreign policy seemed most likely to provide him with the triumph that would salvage his career. His reputation as a statesman remained intact, and he may well have had visions of winning a Nobel Prize when he offered additional reductions in American naval power as a catalyst to the success of the world arms limitation conference meeting in Geneva. Whatever the value of eviscerating the U.S. Navy, such an offer was not likely to throw fear into the hearts of the Japanese militarists. Lest they doubt his peaceful intentions, Hoover authorized the undersecretary of state, William J. Castle, who was notoriously pro-Japanese, to deliver a speech assuring the American people and the Japanese that the United States would back the Hoover-Stimson Doctrine with nothing more than the moral force of public opinion. All Stimson could do was complain to his diary of the tribulations of conducting foreign affairs while working for a pacifist president.

Although the report of the Lytton Commission and Japan's departure from the League were still months away, the crisis in East Asia ended with the Japanese withdrawal from Shanghai. Having established control over Manchuria, most Japanese, military and civilian, were satisfied, even exhilarated. The empire seemed secure, and Japan had stood up to the Western nations, especially America, which persistently denied Japan's demand for equality. A few ideologues, a few publicists, pressed for further expansion, for Japanese hegemony in East Asia, for what was to become Japan's New Order. But these were minor currents in 1932. The military's principal concern was control of Japan, to which end army extremists proceeded to murder and intimidate opposition leaders and to silence its few critics, including those in the military. Japan was lurching toward totalitarianism.

Most Western leaders returned to domestic issues, the economic problems that wracked their nations. Happy to let sleeping dogs lie, some comforted themselves with the notion that the Japanese would eventually recognize the error of their ways. Almost alone, Stimson still brooded. He realized he had angered most Japanese leaders, even those most friendly to the United States. From all sides he was warned against antagonizing them further. But what would happen in a world in which treaty violations went unpunished, in which aggressors feared no reprisals? What were the alternatives to war and appeasement? Was not war with Japan inevitable if the Japanese military went unpunished? And so, within the limits imposed by Hoover, Stimson continued to indict the Japanese for destroying the peace system, for destroying the hopes of men and women of goodwill throughout the world.

Stimson was sometimes plagued by the idea that China's development toward American-style democracy depended upon evidence of the willingness of the United States to come to its aid, to play the role of China's champion. Certainly Chiang Kai-shek and his brother-in-law, Minister of Finance H. H. Kung, envisioned a Japanese-American war that would rescue China. But all Stimson's protests and indictments, however much they irritated the Japanese and worried Hoover and Lamont, did little for China. Some leftist intellectuals professed to see nothing less than Japanese-American collusion, aimed ultimately against the Soviet Union. Closer to the mark were the thoughts of the editor of the *Ta Kung Pao*, China's leading independent newspaper. On behalf of the Chinese people, he thanked Stimson for his efforts—"but they are only words, words, words, and they amount to nothing at all if there is no force to back them."[1] And he realized there would be no force, because the United States and the League had left no doubt that the ideals they espoused would not be backed by force.

Stimson's concerns during the Manchurian crisis clearly had overtones similar to those running through the mind of Philander Knox in 1910: The United States had a special relationship with China, involving an obligation to support Chinese aspirations to be free of imperialist intrusions on its sovereignty. But in addition to that powerful myth, Stimson was confronting the crisis as foreign minister of the world's leading power and groping for a policy appropriate to that role. The enormous increase in America's involvement in world affairs in the 1920s required Stimson and his colleagues to consider their nation's responsibilities. The United States had joined in the creation of a new world order based not only on the League Covenant, but also on the Washington treaties and the Kellogg-Briand Pact. Could Japan be allowed to destroy that order, violate treaty obligations, resort to force and aggression as its military leaders pleased? Stimson wanted to answer that question in the negative, but the restraints on him were consistent with the constraints faced by all American leaders in the postwar world. American responsibility for the new world order did not extend to the use of force: The American commitment to the new order did not extend to risking war.

In East Asia in 1932, the American approach failed. The peace system collapsed. The new world order began to crumble. And China lost Manchuria.

V

While the Japanese settled into Manchuria, two lesser crises in Latin America also stimulated efforts by Stimson on behalf of the new, peaceful world order. Both involved border disputes, one between Bolivia and Paraguay and the other between Peru and Colombia. In both instances one of the parties to the dispute used force to attempt to resolve the issue. In an earlier era, the United States would probably not have been much concerned, so long as no European power was involved. In 1932, after trumpeting the importance of peaceful solutions to international disputes and opposing recognition of territorial claims settled by force in East Asia, Stimson assumed an obligation to address analogous problems in the Western Hemisphere.

In June Bolivian forces overran a Paraguayan post in the Chaco, a beautifully exotic jungle, possession of which would give Bolivia access to the sea—and the possibility of oil. Fighting intensified in the weeks that followed, and Stimson heard the call. There was no danger in the Chaco war of the United States being used by the League, as neither participant belonged to the League. Nor, for that matter, had either signed the Kellogg-Briand Pact. Nonetheless, the principles to which Stimson adhered and of which he had been attempting to persuade the Japanese were at stake. Working through the Union of American Republics, Stimson won a joint nineteen-nation appeal for an end to the fighting—an appeal which concluded with a paraphrase of the Hoover-Stimson Doctrine of nonrecognition. Unfortunately, not even an appeal to principles of the Kellogg Pact, to the renunciation of the use of force to settle controversies, calmed the aggressive instincts of the combatants. The war dragged on, intensified, and did not end until 1935, with all of the Chaco going to Paraguay.

Columbia and Peru had signed the Kellogg Pact, however, and Colombia invoked its provisions a few months after Peru seized the Amazon village of Leticia in September 1932. The Colombian government's reference to the Kellogg Pact came, "coincidentally," with the convening by Stimson of a conference of ambassadors of the Great Powers, which met the day after. Stimson told the ambassadors of his intention to remind Colombia and Peru of their solemn obligation and asked that their governments follow suit. All governments but that of Japan did so, after a fashion. A year and a half later, the League settled the conflict and Colombia regained Leticia.

If Stimson's efforts to preserve the peace system in Latin America were hardly more successful than his efforts in East Asia, the administration did achieve more satisfying results when it could act unilaterally. Hoover was determined to continue the retreat from imperialism in Central America that had begun early in the 1920s. The experience in Nicaragua had enlightened Stimson as to the dangers of interventionism. There were no differences between the president and his secretary of state on this issue.

Hoover did not wait for his inauguration, but instead left shortly after his election on a ten-week, ten-country tour of Latin America. The central theme of his addresses was the intention of the United States to demonstrate that it would be a good—e.g., noninterventionist—neighbor. In 1930 he had the government publish the Clark Memorandum, which denied that the Monroe Doctrine justified intervention, as declared by Roosevelt in his corollary. Although a right to intervene might be claimed for other reasons, the United States would not again assume such a responsibility under the Monroe Doctrine. Similarly, Hoover changed American policy toward recognition, backing away from Wilson's intensely ideological, antirevolutionary criteria. A de facto regime that promised to meet its international obligations and eventually hold elections would be recognized.

Ending the protectorates could also be accomplished largely as an act of will in Washington. Stimson and Hoover were determined to get the U.S. Marines out of Nicaragua, but it took them almost four years. In January 1933, for only the second time in twenty years, there were no American troops in the land of Somoza and Sandino. A similar effort to withdraw from Haiti was thwarted briefly by the Haitian legislature, but occurred shortly after Hoover left office on terms virtually identical to those he and Stimson had stipulated. Perhaps the most ambiguous evidence of American virtue was the persistent refusal to heed the call to intervene in Cuba to depose a vicious dictator, Gerado Machado y Morales, despite the right of intervention granted to the United States by the Cuban Constitution and the 1903 treaty between the two countries. The requisite unrest existed in growing opposition to Machado, but Stimson could stomach no more. He and his advisers chose to perceive no threat to American interests. Intervention would be "intermeddling imperialism of the most flagrant sort."[2] Machado survived to become Franklin Roosevelt's problem.

As Hoover and Stimson prepared to leave office, the United States remained the hegemon of the Caribbean, but the Big Stick advocated by Theodore Roosevelt and used righteously by Woodrow Wilson was no longer in evidence. The scourge of the hemisphere tried to conform to the principles its leaders espoused as they shared in the construction of the postwar peace system. It is worth noting that Hoover and Stimson neither ordered nor threatened intervention in Latin America, despite the fact that during their years in office Latin American governments defaulted on more than $1 million in American loans and confiscated millions of dollars' worth of American property. The empire would have to stand on its own: The marines were not coming.

VI

For seven years, peace organizations all over the world had prepared for the World Disarmament Conference scheduled for February 1932. Delegations from fifty-nine countries appeared for the opening session—which had to be delayed for an hour while the League Council confronted the new crisis caused by Japan's attack on Shanghai. For years the peace movement had pointed toward this conference, the culmination of the postwar effort to bring perpetual peace. The Kellogg-Briand Pact had brought the dream a step closer: Nations committed to the renunciation of war as an instrument of national policy would have little reason to resist the call to reduce their armaments. Slowly the great naval powers had reached agreements, first at Washington in 1921 and 1922 and then at London in 1930. Now, in 1932, naval arms limitation could be extended to other classes of ships, armies could be reduced, land armaments restricted.

The will to peace in the Western democracies was too strong for cynical diplomats to resist. French leaders, still intensely fearful of a revitalized Germany, determined to provide for France's security by obstructing German rearmament and maintaining French military superiority on the continent. No visions of a Heavenly City on earth could shake the French position. France was represented at Geneva, but no more willing to disarm than it had been at any of the naval conferences. The French government had ascertained that it could not depend on American or British support, that it could rely only on its own arms for security. From France there could be little more than the repetition of standard formulas: Somehow the world would first provide for French security and then, only then, was France willing to give serious consideration to disarmament. Nonetheless, France and all those governments that expected little to come of the conference demonstrated their commitment to peace by showing up and hoping to demonstrate to the world that some other government was responsible for the impasse.

In June 1932, after all the familiar arguments and positions had been put forward, after a moderate German government demanding equality for Germany had fallen, Hoover heartened the peace movement with his dramatic proposal for a breakthrough, for the abolition of all offensive weapons and the reduction of remaining weapons by a third. The German, Italian, and Soviet governments responded enthusiastically. The British, French, and Japanese did not. A few weeks later the conference recessed for two months. A few days later, the National Socialist or Nazi party, led by an absurd demagogue named Adolf Hitler, won a plurality in the German elections.

In November Herbert Hoover's prayers for reelection went unanswered. In January 1933 Hitler became chancellor and quickly eliminated the remnants of Weimar democracy in Germany. In February Japan withdrew from the League of Nations. Desperate efforts to save the World Disarmament Conference, to retain the vision of the 1920s, were mounted in Geneva, one after another, by Europeans and Americans alike. But time had run out. The peace movement had failed. In the era of Adolf Hitler and Japanese militarism, a more apocalyptic vision would prevail.

VII

Hoover as president and diplomatist clearly deserved a better fate. He was an abler man than his two immediate predecessors, better informed about the world and its problems, better equipped to be at the helm as the United States expanded its empire and led the world. He was defeated by the Great Depression and Japanese militarism, neither of which he could have prevented.

The world economic crisis and its manifestations in America shadowed his every move. His responses to the Depression were generally but not always unhelpful. His refusal to veto the Smoot-Hawley tariff bill and his long opposition to war debt cancellation exacerbated already grievous situations. His moratorium on war debt and reparations payments came too late to be of much value. Responsibility for collapse of the world economic system cannot be placed on an individual or a single nation, but as the dominant financial power on the globe, the policies of the United States affected other nations enormously. Herbert Hoover, as much as any one man could, had shaped those policies.

Similarly, Japanese militarism long antedated Hoover's presidency—and the Great Depression. Even the specific plans for the Mukden crisis and the takeover of Manchuria had been available since 1927. But Hoover's commendable determination not to use force in support of policy, not to waste the taxpayers' money on military expenditures, sent the Japanese precisely the wrong message. His recognition of the crippling waste of so much of the military budget and his success at the London Conference in 1930 should not obscure the fact that he did not build the U.S. Navy up to treaty limits. The naval limitation treaties of 1922 and 1930 were not evidences of a new world in which navies were no longer needed; they were carefully devised compromises protecting the security and interests of the major naval powers. When one of them, the United States, did not build the ships it was allowed, the balance was destroyed. American interests could no longer be assured of protection, and a power such as Japan, which continued to build, could easily be tempted to adventurism, confident that no potential adversary could—or would—challenge it. Hoover's attitude toward military spending meant that he was the wrong man to lead the United States on a world stage that would have to be shared with Hitler and the Japanese generals.

EPILOGUE

HOOVER'S LEGACY TO ROOSEVELT

For twelve years, Republican statesmen worked closely with business leaders, of whom the most prominent was Lamont, to create a stable world order in which American interests, strategic and economic, would thrive. There was little disposition to use force to this end. A generation that had experienced world war had no appetite for further combat. An active peace movement was quick to rein in any administration that showed signs of lapsing. The government of the United States attempted to restrict other nations to peaceful means of preserving or expanding their interests, of resolving their differences. Washington's vision was of a world in which American influence, based on American financial power, spread quietly and benignly.

In the Republican era, the power and influence of the United States grew throughout the world. This expansion was most evident, most tangible, when measured in terms of economic interests. It was also visible in the efforts of the government to bring stability to Europe and East Asia, as well as to traditional areas of concern in Latin America. Directly or indirectly, Washington participated in nearly every important international meeting of the era, and acted responsibly—with considerable success in achieving American goals.

Before Hoover left office, however, income from international trade and investments had declined sharply. Trade barriers had risen everywhere. The Soviet Union had been the largest importer of American agricultural and industrial products in 1930 and 1931, but in 1932 Soviet leaders sharply reduced purchases from the United States to gain leverage in their quest for American recognition. All over the world the informal empire built on American investments was in jeopardy as capital flowed back to the United States. A new system of international trade and finance would have to be erected on the wreckage of the old. Would it be based on the image of interdependence stressed by Lamont and the Wilsonians of the 1920s—or on economic nationalism and warfare as the jungle of the early 1930s indicated?

Politically, the world scene was no less grim. In Berlin, Hitler was in the Chancellery. Few foresaw the horrors that presence would entail, but it was clear to most of the world's leaders that Hitler was determined to resurrect German power, that the Versailles settlement would not hold—and that whatever their hopes to the contrary, war might be the outcome. In East Asia the worst seemed over, but no one could be sure when the appetite of Japanese imperialists would be whetted again. Even before he entered the White House, the new president, Franklin D. Roosevelt, found Stimson at his door, trying to persuade him to maintain and perhaps intensify pressure on Japan.

The breakdown of the peace system also threatened the formal American empire. Most obvious was the fact that the Philippines were at Japan's mercy, that the American navy was no match for the Japanese in the western Pacific. Congress tried to divest the United States of responsibility for the islands in December 1932, but Hoover's veto delayed that moment. Would the Japanese come after Guam, Wake, Tutuila, Midway? And what of the Hawaiian Islands they had so long coveted? Would a resurrected Germany once again constitute a threat to the hegemony of the United States in the Western Hemisphere? Would the Third Reich seek an empire in the Caribbean as had Kaiser Wilhelm?

Finally, American military forces were not adequate to protect the empire. Throughout the 1920s, in the absence of any serious threats to the overseas interests of the United States, its military power seemed superfluous. The *will* to preserve the empire by peaceful means seemed sufficient to preclude the need for force. The 1930s had begun on a different note. In this darker world the United States could not preserve its security and its broader interests without the willingness to enter into collective security commitments, without creating and using military power. In this darker world that Franklin Roosevelt inherited, there could be no empire without tears.

NOTES

CHAPTER ONE

1. Robert H. Wiebe, *The Search for Order, 1877–1920* (1967), 227.
2. Mira Wilkins, *The Maturing of the Multinational Enterprise: American Business Abroad from 1914 to 1970* (1974), viii.
3. George T. Davis, *A Navy Second to None: The Development of Modern American Naval Policy* (1940), 268.
4. Richard W. Leopold, *The Growth of American Foreign Policy* (1962), 405–6, 426–27.
5. Joan Hoff Wilson, *American Business and Foreign Policy 1920–1933* (1971), x.

CHAPTER TWO

1. Bruce Barton, *The Man Nobody Knows* (1924)
2. Wilson, *American Business and Foreign Policy,* 122, italics added.
3. Wilkins, *Maturing of Multinational Enterprise,* 127.

CHAPTER THREE

1. Roger Dingman, *Power in the Pacific: The Origins of Naval Arms Limitation, 1914–1922* (1976), 140.

CHAPTER FOUR

1. Charles C. Cumberland, *Mexican Revolution: The Constitutionalist Years* (1972), 347.
2. Schurman to Coolidge, April 8, 1924, Jacob Gould Schurman Papers, Collection of Regional History, Cornell University.
3. MacMurray to Kellogg, quoted in Dorothy Borg, *American Policy and the Chinese Revolution, 1925–1928* (1947), 63.

CHAPTER FIVE

1. Quoted by Willys Peck, Consul General, Nanking, January 7, 1933, U.S. Department of State Decimal File 893.00/12284, National Archives.
2. Quoted in Bryce Wood, *The Making of the Good Neighbor Policy* (1961), 57.

SUGGESTIONS FOR FURTHER READING

Three superb essays will serve to introduce the newcomer to the issues and recent literature on the history of the international relations of the 1920s. John Jacobson's "Is There a New International History of the 1920s?" *American Historical Review,* 88 (1983), 617–45, is Europe-centered. John Braeman's "Power and Diplomacy: The 1920s Reappraised," *Review of Politics,* 44 (1982), 342–69, and his surprisingly generous "The New Left and American Foreign Policy During the Age of Normalcy: A Re-examination," *Business History Review,* 57 (1983), 73–104, both focus on American relations worldwide.

If one has time for only a few books from which to gain a quick insight into the contribution of recent scholars to the study of American foreign relations in the 1920s and early 1930s, I recommend the work of Michael J. Hogan, Melvyn P. Leffler, and Joan Hoff Wilson, noted below. Richard W. Leopold, writing without benefit of the monographs of the last twenty-five years, provides the best textbook discussion of the 1920s in his *Growth of American Foreign Policy* (1962). For a useful general history of the period, see Ellis W. Hawley's *The Great War and the Search for a Modern Order.* Hawley stresses the ideas of the "organizational" or "managerial" school of historians. Emily S. Rosenberg, *Spreading the American Dream: American Economic and Cultural Expansion, 1890–1945* (1982), is very thoughtful. An early seminal article on the United States in the 1920s, William Appleman Williams, "The Legend of Isolationism in the 1920s," *Science and Society,* 18 (1954), 1–20, is replete with the brilliant insights and excesses that usually mark his work.

There are a number of useful works focusing on important participants. Wilson is covered well by N. Gordon Levin's *Woodrow Wilson and World Politics* (1968) and John Milton Cooper's *The Warrior and the Priest: Woodrow Wilson and Theodore Roosevelt* (1983). Hughes, or a reasonable facsimile, can be found in Merlo J. Pusey's two-volume *Charles Evans Hughes* (1951), and Betty Glad's "realist" critique, *Charles Evans Hughes and the Illusions of Innocence* (1966)—but see Hughes at work in some of the monographic literature. Hoover gets the attention he deserves in excellent books by Joseph Brandes, *Herbert Hoover and Economic Diplomacy: Department of Commerce Policy, 1921–1928* (1962), and Joan Hoff Wilson, *Herbert Hoover: Forgotten Progressive (1975)*. There is not yet a biography of Lamont, but my *The Chinese Connection: Roger S. Greene, Thomas W. Lamont, George E. Sokolsky and American East Asian Relations* (1978) contains useful material on the man as well as his role in East Asia. Michael Hogan is the principal source for Lamont's activities in Europe. See especially his "Thomas W. Lamont and European Recovery," in Kenneth Paul Jones (ed.), *U.S. Diplomats in Europe, 1919–1941* (1981). For Lamont in Mexico, see Robert Freeman Smith's superb *United States and Revolutionary Nationalism in Mexico, 1916–1932* (1972). Peter Marabell, *Frederick Libby and the American Peace Movement* (1982), is the only book on the most important figure in the peace movement. The standard work on Kellogg is *Frank B. Kellogg and American Foreign Relations, 1925–1929* (1961), by L. Ethan Ellis. Elting E. Morison, in *Turmoil and Tradition* (1960), offers a sensitive sketch of Stimson. Insights into the minds of all these men appear in the studies of the events in which they participated.

Some of the recent works most useful for my discussion of the Harding inheritance were Mira Wilkins, *The Maturing of the Multinational Enterprise: American Business Abroad from 1914–1970* (1974), Robert D. Schulzinger's *The Making of the Diplomatic Mind: The Training, Outlook, and Style of United States Foreign Service Officers 1908–1931* (1975), and articles by Burton I. Kaufman, "The Organizational Dimension of United States Economic Foreign Policy, 1900–1920," *Business History Review*, 46 (1972), 17–44, and Waldo H. Heinrichs, "Bureaucracy and Professionalism in the Development of American Career Diplomacy," in John Braeman et al. (eds.), *Twentieth-Century American Foreign Policy* (1971). For a review of the military in this period, I found George T. Davis, *A Navy Second to None: The Development of Modern American Naval Policy* (1940), valuable and beautifully written. Russell Weigley's *History of the United States Army* (1967) and Alfred Goldberg (ed.), *A History of the United States Air Force 1907–1957* (1957), are the best on their respective services.

On the cultural involvement of the United States abroad, see Rosenberg's *Spreading the American Dream* and Frank Costigliola, *Awkward Dominion: American Political, Economic, and Cultural Re-*

lations with Europe, 1919–1933 (1984). Warren F. Keuhl's *Seeking World Order: The United States and International Organization to 1920* (1969) remains the best approach to the peace movement in the Wilsonian era.

The best source of information on American economic power in the 1920s is the magnificent U.S. Department of Commerce volume, *The United States in the World Economy* (1943), prepared by Hal B. Lary and associates. Nowhere else can all the questions of "how much?" be answered. Without it we are all reduced to vague theorizing. Michael J. Hogan's *Informal Entente: The Private Structure of Cooperation in Anglo-American Economic Diplomacy, 1918–1929* (1977), and Joan Hoff Wilson's *American Business and Foreign Policy, 1920–1933* (1971) are important, as are the Brandes and Wilkins volumes. Still of value are Herbert Feis, *The Diplomacy of the Dollar, 1919–1932* (1950), and Carl Parrini, *Heir to Empire: United States Economic Diplomacy 1916–1923* (1969). See also William H. Becker and Samuel F. Wells, Jr. (eds.), *Economics and American Diplomacy: An Assessment* (1981).

Roger Dingman's *Power in the Pacific: The Origins of Naval Arms Limitation, 1914–1922* (1976) is the single most important book on the Washington Conference. J. Chalmers Vinson's *The Parchment Peace: The United States Senate and the Washington Conference, 1921–1922* (1955) remains useful on domestic politics.

The two most recent studies of the peace movement are Charles Chatfield, *For Peace and Justice: Pacifism in America, 1914–1941* (1971), and Charles DeBenedetti, *Origins of the Modern American Peace Movement* (1978). Marabell's on Libby and Harold Josephson's *James T. Shotwell and the Rise of Internationalism in America* (1975) detail the thoughts of two of the principal leaders of the movement. Robert H. Ferrell, *Peace in Their Time: The Origins of the Kellogg-Briand Pact* (1952), is less sympathetic to the peace organizations and thus an important antidote.

In addition to Smith's *U.S. and Revolutionary Nationalism in Mexico*, I found Karl M. Schmitt's *Mexico and the United States, 1821–1973* (1974) helpful. So were a pair of articles by N. Stephan Kane, "American Businessmen and Foreign Policy: The Recognition of Mexico, 1920–1923," *Political Science Quarterly*, 90 (1975), 293–313, and "Bankers and Diplomats: The Diplomacy of the Dollar in Mexico, 1921–1924," *Business History Review*, 47 (1973), 335–52. For Central America, especially Nicaragua, I continue to find Bryce Wood's *The Making of the Good Neighbor Policy* (1961) eminently sensible.

John L. Gaddis, *Russia, the Soviet Union, and the United States*

(1978), is a *tour de force. Russia and the West under Lenin and Stalin* (1960) by George F. Kennan is still worth a look, as is Robert C. Williams, *Russian Art and American Money, 1900–1940* (1980). For the response to the Chinese revolution, see Akira Iriye, *After Imperialism: The Search for a New Order in the Far East, 1921–1931* (1965), my *Chinese Connection,* and Dorothy Borg's classic *American Policy and the Chinese Revolution, 1925–1928* (1947).

One important catalyst for the explosion of work on the international relations of Europe in the 1920s was Charles S. Maier's *Recasting Bourgeois Europe: Stabilization in France, Germany, and Italy in the Decade after World War I* (1975). Stephen Schuker's *The End of French Predominance in Europe: The Financial Crisis of 1924 and the Adoption of the Dawes Plan* (1976), and Leffler's *The Elusive Quest: America's Pursuit of European Stability and French Security, 1919–1933* are eloquent testimonials to the quality of the best of the recent literature. See also the essays in Jones (ed.), *U.S. Diplomats in Europe, 1919–1941.*

The standard work on the foreign affairs of the Hoover administration remains Robert H. Ferrell's *American Diplomacy During the Great Depression* (1957). Christopher Thorne's massive *The Limits of Foreign Policy: The West, the League and the Far Eastern Crisis of 1931–1933* (1972) swallows the work of dozens of other scholars. Almost everything ever written about the crisis in Manchuria can be found in it. I am probably alone in retaining sympathy for Stimson's efforts. See also Stephen E. Pelz, *Race to Pearl Harbor: The Failure of the Second London Naval Conference and the Onset of World War II* (1974).

INDEX

ABOUT THE AUTHOR

WARREN I. COHEN, professor of history at Michigan State University, is a specialist in American relations with East Asia. He was a Fulbright lecturer in Tokyo in 1969–70, and has served as editor of the scholarly quarterly, *Diplomatic History*. His published work includes *The American Revisionists* (1967), *The Chinese Connection* (1978), and *Dean Rusk* (1980), a critical study of the diplomacy of the American secretary of state in the 1960s. He is also the author of the standard survey of U.S. relations with China, *America's Response to China* (2nd edition, 1980).

A NOTE ON THE TYPE

The rest of this book was set on the Linotype in Aster, a type face designed by Francesco Simoncini (born 1912 in Bologna, Italy) for Ludwig and Mayer, the German type foundry. Starting out with the basic old-face letter forms that can be traced back to Francesco Griffo in 1495, Simoncini emphasized the diagonal stress by the simple device of extending diagonals to the full height of the letter forms and squaring off. By modifying the weights of the individual letters to combat this stress, he has produced a type of rare balance and vigor. Introduced in 1958, Aster has steadily grown in popularity.

A NOTE ON THE TYPE